THE FEMALE SALES LEADER.

THE FEMALE SALES LEADER.

Empowering Women to Lead in Sales and Tech

LUCY WILLIAMS - JONES

MARINA AYTON   PENNY ORME

with foreword from
Andy Whyte

**MEDDICC
MEDIA**

For the women who have been underestimated, overlooked, or told to wait their turn.

For the trailblazers who refused to accept "no" as the final answer.

For the next generation of fearless leaders who will redefine what's possible.

And for every ally committed to building a world where talent, ambition, and leadership know no gender.

This book is for you.

Lucy, Marina & Penny

MEDDICC MEDIA

ISBN: 978-1-0369-1349-6

MEDDICC Ltd
2 The Crescent
Wisbech
Cambridgeshire
United Kingdom
PE13 1EH

http://www.meddicc.com

CONTENTS

FOREWORD

ANDY WHYTE – CEO OF MEDDICC

It isn't lost on me the sense of irony that comes with being a man writing the foreword for this book. When I was asked, my initial impression was that it was counterintuitive. But as I reflected, I realized that this very discomfort – the feeling of uncertainty of whether it's my place is exactly why men need to be part of this conversation.

The truth is, the challenges women face in sales leadership aren't women's challenges – they're industry-wide challenges. Solving them requires everyone, regardless of gender, to step up.

The idea for this book struck me during a webinar where Lucy, Marina, Penny, and our CRO, Pim, discussed the often-overlooked leap from being an individual contributor to stepping into a first sales leadership role. Lucy made a comment that stayed with me: "There are no books to help someone make the transition from IC to leadership." While that was true, I realized that there was an even bigger issue. If we want more women in sales, it begins with having more women in sales leadership.

Representation matters. Aspiring saleswomen need leaders they can look to and see themselves in. They need role models to inspire them to grow into leadership and show them it is possible.

Without those leaders paving the way, the progress we need will remain out of reach.

So, I asked Marina, Penny, and Lucy if they'd consider helping address this gap by writing this book. Without hesitation, they said yes, diving into a project that turned out to be much more demanding than any of us initially anticipated. Their dedication – giving their time and expertise with no reward other than the hope of inspiring future sales leaders is remarkable. Their selflessness and commitment leaves me feeling genuinely moved.

Yet, reading their words has been both inspiring and, at times, uncomfortable. As a man, it was hard to confront the challenges Lucy, Marina, and Penny talk about – the subtle biases and the lack of representation. But what struck me most is how the authors approached these issues. Instead of assigning blame, they have provided thoughtful, constructive feedback and practical guidance for navigating and overcoming these challenges. Their writing isn't accusatory – it's empowering, and that is what I believe will make this book required reading for decades to come.

At MEDDICC, we often include a metaphor in our new customer kick-off presentations: a cartoon of a man panning for gold, representing a bad salesperson sifting aimlessly for success. Alongside, we showcase a professional salesperson to highlight the traits that set them apart. To personalize the session, we ask for a headshot of a high-performing saleswoman from the customer's team. Across over 500 kick-offs, the responses have always been one of two: "Absolutely, I know just the person," or "I'm afraid we don't have any."

Not once has the answer been, "Our female salespeople aren't high performers." This isn't about talent – it's about opportunity, visibility, and intention. There's no excuse for the absence of high-performing women in any sales team, and that is why this book matters.

Through their experiences, Lucy, Marina, and Penny provide not just a roadmap for aspiring female leaders but also a challenge for all of us in the industry. If we want more women in sales, we need to create environments where women are consistently promoted into leadership, inspiring others to see sales not just as a stepping stone but as a long-term career to aspire to. It's about building workplaces where talent can thrive, where bias is dismantled, and where diversity isn't just a value – it's a priority.

Whether you are a leader, a mentor, an individual contributor, or simply someone who wants to make a difference, this book is a call to action.

It's time to ensure that the answer to "Do you have a high-performing female salesperson?" is always, "Yes, many!"

To Lucy, Marina, and Penny: thank you for your courage, your generosity, and your commitment to the next generation of sales leaders.

To everyone else: We've got work to do! LFG!

ABOUT THE AUTHORS

If working on this book, speaking to 26 external contributors, male and female, across 20+ organizations, has taught us anything, it's the significance of hearing a range of voices on a topic. Each of us is at a different stage of sales leadership, and none of us took the same route to get to where we are. Our hope is that each reader will gel with at least one of us, and that every person who reads this will benefit from our varied experiences. And so, to give some context as to why we know what we're talking about, let us introduce ourselves:

LUCY WILLIAMS – JONES

When I started my career in tech sales 25 years ago, the industry looked very different. Women in the sales teams and leadership were few and far between. But I was determined. Determined to succeed, to consistently perform at the top of my game, and ultimately to lead – so that I could help others do the same.

I fell into the world of tech at eighteen years old in my gap year, when I decided that I should earn some money before starting university in Manchester to study sports science. That year was amazing, I learned a lot of new skills and found out I really enjoyed the job and the chase of being an individual contributor. I have been fortunate to work at five amazing companies, three of which have become public and met some great people along the way.

Moving into leadership wasn't just a career move for me, it was a calling. I wanted to pay forward to the talented young sales people coming up through the ranks, to give them the tools, insights, and confidence to build successful careers of their own. Because a career in sales isn't just about hitting targets – it's about creating opportunities, forging relationships, and designing a life you love to live.

Sales to me is much like chess – a game of strategy, foresight, and adaptability. I've always been passionate about the mental discipline required in both. You have to anticipate your prospects' moves, counter objections, and position your product as the best solution – all while managing the timing of your 'checkmate' (the close). Plus, just like in chess, every deal is different, and you have to base your play and moves on your opponent, the customer.

But beyond the strategy, sales is about people. It's about emotional intelligence – knowing how to read a room, understand a client's unspoken needs, and build trust. This book isn't just about the mechanics of sales leadership and driving diversity across teams, it's the human side of it. The lessons we have learnt, the challenges we have faced and the mindset shifts we have adopted to help us grow, not just as professionals but as people.

I live in the Cotswolds, with my husband Aj, my biggest champion and our little cavapoo Beau. Life is full, busy and rewarding in more ways than I could ever have imagined when I first started out (more so over the past two years, writing this book). And that's exactly what I hope this book helps others achieve – a career that enables them to live their best lives, both professionally and personally.

Outside of work you'll often find me exploring the countryside, visiting new continents, trying to track down the perfect Sunday roast or with my nose in a book with a glass of wine, soaking up new knowledge. Learning is something that keeps me sharp, and being able to apply the learnings in real life situations gives me a buzz.

To every woman in tech sales who has ever wondered if she belongs at the table, you do. And I hope this book helps you claim your seat with confidence.

MARINA AYTON

My journey into sales began unexpectedly. After graduating from university, I found myself drawn to the energy of a small, scrappy startup. This early experience, navigating the challenges of building something from the ground up, instilled in me a deep appreciation for hard work, resilience, and the importance of customer-centricity.

Since then, I've had the privilege of working with a diverse range of technology organizations, from high-growth startups to established enterprises listed on the NASDAQ 100. This exposure has provided me with a unique perspective on the evolving sales landscape and the importance of adaptability, continuous learning, and just being a good person.

Growing up in a family of entrepreneurs, I was instilled with a strong work ethic and a drive to succeed. Dinners at home often felt like "Dragons' Den," with lively discussions and a focus on entrepreneurial pursuits. My own early ventures – selling steel-reinforced fiberglass cherry blossom trees (yes, you read that right!) and later, London Velvet and Pink Diesel – taught me valuable lessons about sales, perseverance, and the importance of understanding customer needs and running a successful business.

Throughout my career, I'm proud that I've consistently exceeded expectations, achieving over 200% of quota annually for the last eight years, with a peak of nearly 700% in one year. Every year I have pushed myself to do things and take risks that I never thought I would have – and thankfully, most have paid off. Now, as a leader, I take immense pride in my team's success, with the best years seeing every member of the team reach the President's Club – witnessing the growth and development of the team.

I hope to create environments where individuals feel safe to fail, try new things, take risks, feel valued and are empowered to reach their full potential.

My experiences in these various companies have offered valuable insights into both effective and ineffective leadership. I've learned that fostering a diverse and inclusive environment is crucial for building high-performing teams, while toxic environments can significantly hinder growth and success. While I don't claim to have all the answers, I've reflected on these lessons and hope to share my insights and experiences with you through this book.

Outside of work, I am a highly competitive individual, always striving to improve myself and those around me – you'll find me on a tennis court, a netball pitch, or enjoying a ski slope whenever possible. I am also an avid reader, something I have forced myself to adopt (and now love!) while growing up with the challenges of dyslexia.

PENNY ORME

I never had a clear career path in mind as a child – I just knew I wanted one and that I wanted to be successful. Growing up in the '80s and '90s, hard work and ambition were celebrated, and my incredible mum instilled in me the drive to stand on my own two feet. It wasn't just about financial success; it was about proving to myself that I was capable.

After earning a degree in Archaeology & Classics (not the most obvious route into sales!), I landed in London and started in publishing, but it was the buzz of the advertising sales team that drew me in. Making 80 calls a day, chasing targets, and winning deals – I was hooked. That was the start of a successful 30-year sales career spanning financial services and software, from enterprise sales roles to VP and CRO positions at companies like Meta, iManage, SUSE, and Causeway Technologies.

Throughout my career, I have often been the only woman in the room – whether in sales teams, leadership meetings, and on Exec teams. Despite that, I've built a successful career, kicking off my first year in enterprise sales I was awarded *'Global Rookie of the Year'* bringing in $10m followed by a further 10 consecutive years as a top performer at Merrill, being recognized as a *Top 10 EMEA Sales Leader* for three consecutive years by Sales Confidence, and, more recently, named one of Pavilion's *50 CROs to Watch*. I've successfully completed over 100 quarters, all while raising two children and navigating challenges that many women have faced in their careers (as I discovered in writing this book). At the time, I worried about the potential negative impact of having children on my career. I had spent years building momentum, and the fear of losing my edge or being seen as less committed was real, but I – and so many other women – have proven that it's absolutely possible to thrive in both career and motherhood. Sales has given me incredible opportunities, from negotiating multi-million-pound deals and traveling the world to working alongside brilliant people and mentoring the next generation of sales talent.

But my story isn't unique – there are so many talented women in sales who have the potential to thrive, and I want to see more of them in leadership roles. Turning 50 has been a moment of reflection, bringing into focus the things I'm truly passionate about – championing diversity in sales, supporting women on their path to leadership, and helping organizations build more inclusive cultures.

I've had the privilege of working with some of the very best sales professionals – many of whom are women – and I would love to see more women pursue and succeed in sales. Working with Lucy and Marina on this book has been a privilege, and I hope it sparks conversation, challenges perspectives, and – no matter how small – helps drive meaningful change.

Outside of work, I live in Buckinghamshire with my husband Marcus – my inspiration and biggest supporter – our two teenagers (Max and Amelie), and our crazy boxer dog, Dotty. We love traveling, skiing, and supporting Tottenham Hotspur FC (which, let's be honest, is quite tough at the moment!).

The Female Sales Leader was written with the help of Robin Daly and published by MEDDICC.

PREFACE

In 2022, the three of us were included in a panel to talk about the shift from being an Individual Contributor in the world of technology sales to leading a team. Between us we found we had a range of tenures, stories, and routes to leadership. As we swapped our stories and experiences, we noticed a commonality in some of the challenges and opportunities we have faced in our careers. Some of these stories were shocking and funny in equal parts, and so we joked we should write a book about them. That's where the idea for *The Female Sales Leader* began.

We are at such a crucial moment in tech sales – its current growth and evolution presents people with a chance to put themselves in a position that allows them to grow and flourish. Now more than ever before, there's an opportunity for anyone, regardless of gender, race, or sexuality to be successful – especially because a lot of tech companies are really driving inclusivity and diversity through initiatives.

The role of women in leadership, particularly in sales, has evolved significantly. As of 2024, 34% of VPs and 29% of C-suite leaders are women[1] – more than ever before, but in tech sales, the gender gap persists. In 2021, women made up only 28.8% of software sales reps[2], despite comprising 48% of entry-level positions in the workforce[3]. Women are advancing in leadership roles, but not at the same rate as their male peers. Moreover, many women leave companies before reaching the C-suite.

While systemic barriers remain, there's reason for hope. DEI initiatives and women's leadership networks are creating more opportunities. And the business case for diversity is clear: the more diverse an organization is, the more profitable. This makes it not only a moral imperative, but a strategic advantage.

The goal of this book is threefold. First, to highlight – through stories and experiences from both us and 26 contributors from across the tech industry – why women should consider a career in sales. Second, to provide guidance on how to build a long and successful career in the field. And third, to outline the steps organizations, leaders, and peers can take to create an inclusive, gender-diverse environment that drives success for individuals, teams, and companies alike.

PENNY: My motivation for this book is simple: I want to inspire more women to see tech sales as a fantastic career choice and shine a light on the challenges many face along the way. Through the stories and insights that Marina, Lucy, and I share – along with the experiences of the many incredible men and women who contributed – I hope this book not only informs but also sparks conversation and real change.

There's no doubt progress has been made. Equal pay and DE&I initiatives are finally at the forefront, and more companies are recognizing the value of diverse teams. But despite these efforts, the number of women in sales leadership – particularly in the C-suite – remains stubbornly low. During our research, it became clear that many of the same challenges persist, from bias in hiring and promotions to the pressures of balancing career and family.

What I didn't expect was just how many women had experienced similar struggles to the ones I have had. In some ways, it was reassuring to know I wasn't alone, but it was also frustrating to see how common these barriers still are. That's why this book isn't just about storytelling – it's about learning from real experiences, reflecting on the research, and understanding what we can all do differently.

Whether you're a woman in sales carving out your path, a leader looking to create a more inclusive culture, or an ally wanting to make a difference, my hope is that this book helps you recognize the challenges, question the status quo, and take meaningful steps toward change.

LUCY: By sharing my experiences and view as to what a great industry we work within, I am hoping we can encourage more women into tech and more specifically sales. I really hope this book helps alleviate the worry of them being the only one.

There has been a change in the industry over the past 5-10 years and there are more women than ever before, but it's not perfect. If we are able to get more women into sales roles, which leads to more women in sales leadership positions, we can shape the industry and make it a better place.

Gender diversity isn't just about conversation – it's a catalyst for change. The future of tech sales will be shaped by diverse voices, fresh perspectives and inclusive leadership. When we bring more women into the room, we don't just change the numbers, we change the game. This isn't just about meeting quotas, it's about unlocking potential, driving innovation, and building a stronger, more dynamic industry for the next generation.

For me, being involved in this has been such a great experience to work with other women who have all been through the same challenges, yet reaped the same successes within the tech industry. I really hope the insights we share from a rounded viewpoint of working in Tech Sales can help shape the future for many for years to come. This is not just about being a woman in sales, as Penny said, it is about sharing our viewpoint with all to make a difference to everyone, and make the largest impact. Having more diversity in sales will help shape the future and that it's a great career where they can thrive.

MARINA: My goal in writing this book is to inspire more women to consider a career in tech sales. This industry offers incredible opportunities for intellectual growth and personal development. It's challenging, yes, but it's rarely just a job. It's intellectually stimulating, demanding, and incredibly rewarding. And while it's still male-dominated, that presents a unique opportunity for women to break barriers and have a significant impact. We can bring our unique perspectives and leadership styles to the table and reshape the landscape of tech sales.

This book is for those who are curious, ambitious, and ready to take on a challenge. You'll learn valuable skills, from navigating complex organizations to handling difficult situations with confidence. You'll also discover that you're not alone on this journey. By sharing my own experiences and insights, I hope to empower you to embrace the opportunities that await you in the exciting world of tech sales.

For anyone picking up this book, there's a lot you can learn. It will illustrate what can be gained from a career in sales, particularly for women, and how it will allow you to grow and develop yourself. Whether you're starting out in your sales career or you're looking into the next step, with this book you can learn from three people who have made a lot of mistakes, but simultaneously some quite good decisions.

With the ultimate goal of getting more women into sales leadership, we will explore how women can deal with the obstacles that come with working in a male-dominated workplace, and rise through the ranks while still thriving in their personal lives.

OUR EXTERNAL CONTRIBUTORS ON WHY DIVERSITY MATTERS TO THEM AND WHY THEY CONTRIBUTED TO THE FEMALE SALES LEADER

ADAM QUARTERMAINE
SVP EMEA | HARNESS

Throughout my career I have been truly blessed to work with incredible female sales and leadership talents; the consistent levels of overachievement from these women has been breathtaking. Much progress has been made to attract more women into technology and leadership, but so much more needs to happen and soon. It's a big win for every stakeholder involved in building and operating world class companies.

ALICE CARLISLE
REGIONAL VICE PRESIDENT | WIZ

In a world where everyone is different, and in sales where people really are at the heart of what we do, balancing a team with diversity from all perspectives brings in the humanity and reality to a team. Ensuring that younger generations can look and see people who are similar to them achieving great things and allowing them to be inspired is critically important, we must continue to pay forward what many generations before us have worked hard to achieve.

EMMA MULQUEENY OBE
HEAD OF ESG | CAUSEWAY

Diversity in any career is important, but in leadership, it's essential. As I've advanced, real support has been hard to find. Training is often outdated, designed for men, or lazily adapted with a pink wash and a few "...or women" add-ons. Assumptions persist – women handle 'fluffy' sales while men close deals, or women don't understand tech. Worse, some women in leadership kick down rather than lift others up. That's why this book, and the women behind it, matter.

Women frequently leave sales as they climb the ladder. They're overlooked for promotions, locked out of the 'boys' club' after career breaks, and burned out from working twice as hard for less pay. Yet, women excel at sales. The long-game nature of modern sales plays to our strengths. Invest in strong leadership mentors for women, and you'll see them thrive.

I contributed to this book because I believe in its message. My hope is that it gives women both inspiration and a clear path to success. Ultimately, we need parity, in pay, in opportunity, and in the way leadership is developed.

FIONA MCCLUNE
CRO | STRUCTUREFLOW

Diversity matters because it drives progress, connection, and peace. As a woman born in the 70s, navigating a male-dominated tech sales world as a gay woman, I've seen how hard it is to find space. It wasn't just about getting a seat at the table – it was about being seen for who I truly am.

Kindness and equality are the only ways to true peace. Respecting each individual's dignity creates a space where everyone can bring their whole selves to work, without fear of judgment or exclusion. Without this, we can't innovate or collaborate effectively.

Choosing not to support diversity, or turning a blind eye to the struggles of underrepresented groups, is complicit behavior. Silence and indifference harm, just as much as active discrimination. True strength comes from embracing our differences and building environments where everyone belongs. Only then can we create real peace.

FLAVIA BROWN
AREA VICE PRESIDENT | MULTIVERSE

Studying politics and learning more about feminism sparked my passion for equality. In my early 20s, I was surrounded by talented and driven female friends who, in nearly all cases, outshone their male counterparts. This made me question why such a significant gender imbalance persisted in business and leadership roles. Now, in my early 30s and as a mother, I better understand the challenges women face, particularly the barriers to returning to work and advancing in male-dominated fields like sales. When the opportunity arose to contribute to the book, I was eager to get involved. I want to champion women entering sales early in their careers and support mothers in ensuring they are set up for success when returning to work.

HANNAH AJIKAWO
CEO & FOUNDER | REVENUE FUNNEL

Diversity matters because when we ignore – whether intentionally or not – the voices and experiences of those who are different to us, we miss out on vital pieces to the puzzles that we are trying to solve in life and business. Every story matters because it's another perspective. I contributed to the book because female sales leaders are still far and few between. We still appear to be the underdogs, the "risky hire" and there are far too many examples of exceptional women in sales for us to still hold these archaic views. If I can help to continue a new dialogue about what it means to be a female sales leader then I"m always going to raise my hands and get in the mix.

HANNAH BATES
MAJOR GLOBAL AE | DATADOG

When Lucy asked me to be part of an initial panel discussion to share my own experiences of being a female in tech I jumped at the opportunity! *The Female Sales Leader* is a book I wish I had access to at the beginning of my career 15 years ago. It would have been an invaluable resource for navigating the challenges I faced as a young woman entering the tech industry straight out of University. I am deeply passionate about working within diverse teams, as bringing together individuals from various backgrounds fosters a rich array of perspectives, ideas, and problem-solving approaches. This diversity is instrumental in driving success, not only for teams but also for individual contributors. Looking ahead, I would love to participate in meetings where women are no longer in the minority but represent the majority.

HAZEL KOCH
MAJORS AE | ZSCALER

Representation is powerful. As one of the few women in the room for most of my career, I know how important it is to see diverse leaders shaping decisions. Diverse teams drive better outcomes – different perspectives fuel innovation, stronger customer relationships, and better sales results. Yet, tech and sales remain dominated by one demographic, and that needs to change. Bias exists, whether we see it or not, and breaking that cycle starts with inclusive environments where people feel valued and can grow. When companies prioritize diversity, they foster mentorship, challenge outdated norms, and create spaces where everyone thrives. I want to be part of that shift.

JASON CREANE
VP & GENERAL MANAGER | VARONIS

If we prioritize creating a diverse workforce, which has shared values, then we can create a more engaging and inclusive culture. We also attract a greater pool of talent, boost retention, and generate more success for our people and our customers.

Contributing to this book was important to me because I enjoy working with a more diverse workforce and I have seen the tangible benefits when we prioritized it. When I focus on it, I can create these benefits within our company, but if we were all to focus on it, we could create these benefits across an entire industry.

JOSH REINER
VP EMEA | WIZ

A diverse team should be the core of any go-to-market strategy you develop. I often use Peter Drucker's famous quote, "Culture eats strategy for breakfast" when articulating the importance of culture while executing Wiz's strategy across EMEA. No matter how detailed and solid our strategy is, if you don't have diverse sets of ideas and an environment that welcomes new ideas, your likelihood of failure increases. Inevitably, you will have challenges thrown at you, and how employees act in these critical situations often determines the outcome. Even with all the advancement of technology, it still comes down to the people who are responsible for executing Wiz's values and those values are built on diversity.

KATE HUNT
REGIONAL DIRECTOR | SALESFORCE

Diversity is about creating a world where everyone feels seen, heard, and valued. Your voice matters, and your perspective is vital. As women navigating this bold, evolving world – and as working mothers balancing careers while shaping the next generation – we have a responsibility to challenge limits, unlock opportunities, and keep the doors open for those who follow. My contribution to this book is a heartfelt step towards inspiring women to live their lives with meraki – with soul, creativity, and love – and to embrace their power and realize their limitless potential.

KATHRYN POOL
SENIOR DIRECTOR, HEAD OF ENTERPRISE RE-TAIL INDUSTRY | MICROSOFT UK

Diversity is essential. It enriches and brings balance to our working lives. Drawing on my own career journey, I recognizethe importance of challenging existing norms and encouraging new approaches to promote diversity in the workplace. Diversity fuels diversity, and thus it is our responsibility, through supporting such initiatives as this book, to continue to advance awareness of the need for diversity and inclusion both now and in the future.

LAURA LENTI
VP EMEA | NEPTUNE SOFTWARE

I grew up in a modest family in Rome, Italy. When my father passed away as a child I felt responsible for my family; I dreamed of improving our financial situation so we would never have to worry.

I had the ambition to change our future. As a young girl, I needed mentorship and direction, yet women's potential was often overlooked. Even today, women remain underrepresented in technology, sales, and leadership.

I contributed to this book because I want young women to know what's possible – to dream big, seek guidance, and have role models who've navigated the challenges before them. I became a leader to create opportunities for others, to be the mentor I never had, and to help build diverse workplaces where everyone can thrive.

LYNDSEY REES-POWLES
AVP DIGITAL SALES | SPLUNK

I am really lucky to have such a diverse team of individuals from different backgrounds and experiences who bring different ideas and perspectives. This encourages creativity and drives growth and innovation. Having diversity creates greater empathy and understanding which enhances team morale as it creates an inclusive environment with greater collaboration.

I wanted to contribute to *The Female Sales Leader* because I'm passionate about encouraging more women into sales. This book shares experiences and insights from the best in the business and will hopefully inspire women that are thinking of a career in Tech sales or are navigating through their careers. My 1st leader took a chance on me and really shaped my journey to be a female sales leader and I wanted to be able to do the same for others.

MARK DANDO
GM, EMEA NORTH | SUSE

When I look back on my career in sales and commercial leadership, one of my biggest learnings is that building a diverse team isn't just a nice to have, it's a strategic imperative. In my early roles, I was surrounded by people who looked and thought just like me (and this was my approach to building teams!) and whilst we've made progress since then, we're far from where we need to be. I've had the privilege of working alongside exceptional women in sales who consistently challenge conventional thinking and forge deeper client relationships, often resulting in them outperforming their male counterparts. I think what the MEDDICC team are doing with *The Female Sales Leader* is really important and I was delighted to make a small contribution. I'm passionate about the subject area because building world-class sales organizations demands different perspectives, experiences, and approaches. We need to keep this conversation going until diversity in sales leadership isn't just an initiative, but our standard way of operating.

MELISSA DI DONATO
CEO & CHAIR | KYRIBA

As a female leader in the still male-dominated technology industry, equality of opportunity is one of my biggest priorities. I've seen first-hand that diversity and inclusion are not just buzzwords but key drivers of business success. While it's encouraging to see an increasing number of female leaders, as well as those from diverse backgrounds, we still face significant challenges and must continue to push for progress so women have equal access to opportunities in all industries, especially STEM. I'm committed to continuing this journey and challenging the status quo so our workforce better reflects the rich diversity of our global economy. I hope this book serves as a tool to educate and inspire my fellow leaders from all backgrounds to be an agent for the change that is so direly needed.

OLLIE SHARPE
CRO | TRUMPET

I love the sales industry, but there are a few areas where we need to improve it! One of those is diversity. Only 29% of tech sales professionals are female and less than 50% of females believe that their company is doing all they can to attract female talent. The ironic thing is that diverse workforces are more successful! We need to make sales a more welcoming place to attract more females and if we had more female leaders then it would make a huge difference – and that is down to us to change the sales industry.

PETE CROSBY
CRO | REVELESCO

The best teams operate, execute and win because they place diversity as their foundation on which to build. Whether it is diversity of background, of ethnicity, of age, of gender, of whatever; leaders have a duty to build teams that win. It is ridiculous in the 21st century that we even need to be debating this, but we do, and this book is an essential tool for navigating the discussion, and for enabling leaders to set women up for success.

RICH PEREZ
RVP, NEMEA | GRAFANA LABS

As a father of three, two of which are girls, married to an amazing woman who has built a career in technology, I have an ingrained personal interest in seeing a stronger opportunity for women in technology. Sales is a career which provides rewards to many, and I have been fortunate to be part of, and lead, diverse teams over my career. That has always provided insight into the value which can be derived by empowering individuals with different backgrounds and perspectives in the group. When a challenge arises, what better way to create a solution than with people who see the world differently, yet hold the same shared goal? Diversity in technology sales should not be an option: It should be by design.

RONAL KARIA
VP OF SALES (CENTRAL AND NORTHERN EUROPE) | SLACK

Diversity is not something that is important today in the workplace but something we have to fix for generations to come. It starts with each of us making it a priority and as a leader supporting the talent around us irrespective of their age/sex/background/color etc...

More now than ever having different perspectives and views allows businesses to form a better view of their customer needs. As a leader the best teams I have led are ones with a balance of diversity!

STEPHANIE MCLAURIN
HEAD OF SALES | BIRDIE

The business benefits are well known – organizations with greater diversity among their executive teams tend to have higher profits and longer-term value. Reducing the gender pay gap could add between $12 and $28 trillion to global GDP. It's a win-win for us all.

But diversity is only the beginning. For companies to benefit from diversity of thought we have to create the space for challenge.

I have been fortunate enough to work with a number of coaches and mentors over the years who have equipped me with the tools, the confidence and the courage to speak up and to challenge. This is why I was so grateful to be asked to contribute to this book – I have the hope that this book gives other women the tools, the confidence and the courage to speak up and support allies with their desire to create space for challenge.

THEA PETCH
CLIENT DIRECTOR | SNOWFLAKE

Diversity matters because it drives innovation, challenges conventional thinking, and creates an environment where everyone can thrive. From my experience working across complex data and AI projects, in sports, and as a mum, I've seen how diverse teams bring unique perspectives to problem-solving, leading to better solutions and stronger outcomes. Contributing to this book was an opportunity to share my thoughts on why women are, and will continue to be, exceptional leaders.

PART ONE

WHY TECH?
WHY SALES?
WHY YOU?

Our initial motivation for writing this book was clear from the beginning: we want to get more women into tech sales and into sales leadership. But this isn't just about women – it's about shifting perspectives across the industry. Men and others in leadership roles play a crucial part in creating inclusive environments that support diverse teams. This part serves as the first step in that direction: convincing you, the reader, to join us in reshaping the landscape of sales.

In this part, we will lay out the reasons why you should consider a career in tech, and more specifically, in sales. We look at the things that attracted us to our careers, as well as what has made us such advocates for this industry.

Throughout this part you will see why women are particularly suited to sales and sales leadership – and why organizations should be embracing them for the overall success of their teams.

Along with that, you will leave with an initial understanding of what makes a great leader, and why people choose to move into leadership.

Chapter One

WHY TECHNOLOGY?

In a survey on tech leadership, Deloitte said it best: technology used to power the business, but now, it is the business. The tech industry is one that is constantly shifting and growing; no one wants to be left behind, and its transformative power means that demand for technology has increased across businesses.[4] As a result, tech budgets are steadily increasing, from an average 3.64% of revenue to 5.49% in 2023.[5] It is a constantly growing industry; in 2022, the US tech sector added close to 260,000 jobs, the most in a single year since 2000,[6] a number that is projected to rise to over 300,000 in 2024.[7] In the UK, the amount of entry-level tech roles saw a 127% rise in 2022.[8]

Just look at the meteoric rises of unicorn SaaS companies – privately-held start-ups that are valued over $1 billion that are set on an upward trajectory. They have rapid growth plans, and the internal growth and revenue to support it. The tremendous growth in the industry comes with increased investment; from 2017 to 2022, for example, fast-growing UK tech companies raised nearly £100 billion.[9] In the US, 64% of venture capital investment was in tech in 2022.[10] There has never been a better time to pursue a career in tech – especially as we witness the explosive growth of generative AI; a majority of professionals expect that their organizations will invest more in AI in the coming years.[11] As AI progresses, it will undoubtedly fuel further growth and development in the industry, one that is unbelievably exciting to be a part of, with many opportunities both for your career and personal development. When people think of tech, their minds often go to giants like Google or Meta before considering B2B tech as a lucrative career option. Despite that, B2B tech is an industry that allows you to thrive and have an incredibly rewarding career. So, why should you consider a career in tech?

CONTINUOUS INNOVATION

PENNY: *What brought me to technology was quite simple: it is the future. Early on in my career I witnessed the rise of the dot-com boom, and got a glimpse into the impact fast growth technology had on the markets. It was a new era of entrepreneurs! As B2B software sales evolved I knew I wanted to be a part of it and have never looked back.*

Tech companies are forging a new frontier, creating products and services that support and reshape the industry and world around us. From streaming to security, many of us can think of a technological innovation that completely shifted the way we do things: from Deliveroo to exercise tracking apps like Strava. Tech is constantly changing; think of the iPod. When it was launched in 2001, it completely transformed the way people listened to music, jump-starting the rise of digital music. In 2006, it was responsible for 40% of Apple's overall revenue.[12] However, with the rise of the smartphone, the demand for iPods began to decrease. In 2014, only 1.25% of Apple's revenue was attributed to the iPod. By 2022, Apple had discontinued it in all forms. This demonstrates for us that what might seem like a tech staple now could be obsolete in ten years.

The constant evolution in tech provides an incredible opportunity for those involved: to not only have a sneak preview into what's coming next but to have the ability to form it ourselves, truly support transformation both for organizations but as individuals as well.

As the tech industry continues to grow, so too does the opportunity it holds for you; because it is a rapid growth market, there lies serious potential for career growth. It only takes looking at the lightning speed at which AI is developing to understand how the tech landscape could transform in the next ten years, and the same can be said for your career. The nature of the level of investment and innovation seen in tech means there are new companies and scale-ups created every year – the opportunity is exponential.

Success in this industry is about being nimble and able to pivot quickly, which means it remains especially interesting and provides a constant learning opportunity. Within it, you can be part of something truly disruptive, that changes the way we do things forever, and that can be invigorating.

DEVELOPMENT

Learning new things and being developed are key criteria for a stimulating and interesting career. The very nature of the tech industry is that it is constantly changing, and as a result you are on the cutting edge of innovation and never stop learning or developing. With this comes opportunity. Developing yourself – whether that be self learning or through your company – having an 'always learning' and curious mind is essential for career growth and personal development. Choosing the right company can accelerate your growth, providing you with training opportunities and great expertise on the job.

A lot of accomplished sales people cut their teeth at playbook companies – companies that use a structure and a strategy to drive consistent performance, achieve repeatable sales success and scale operations. A playbook company allows both new starters and experienced sales professionals to have one standard process across various functions that provides a recipe for success. Some playbook companies include Snowflake, Wiz, DataDog and MongoDB.

There are structured processes from pipeline generation all the way to the closing of the deal and beyond in playbook companies. While they can be quite intense, with transparency on leading indicators and performance, their structured approach can enhance performance across teams and foster a culture of consistency and constant improvement.

MARINA: *Working for a playbook company feels like attending a university for sales. It provides the essential processes and structure needed for achieving repeatable success. For me it's always provided a compass to keep me on track and ensure I am educating my customers with the best way to buy technology. What I truly appreciate about this approach – and why I passionately advocate for it – is that it transforms the art of selling into a science. Having a framework empowers sales people to effectively guide customers through the buying process, making it easier for them to choose the right software solutions for their pains and needs.*

LUCY: *I started working for a true playbook company when I joined BMC in 2014. This was an intentional move from my side and something that I purposely sought out as I had heard so much* *about others' successes. The opportunity I was lucky enough to be part of allowed me to learn how to implement a solid process, but also gave me the ability to learn from the best in the industry. I have been really fortunate to work with some amazing leaders, as well as sales professionals, which makes every day a learning day. Although all the companies I have worked for are different, and solve different client challenges, the playbook is the same. The streamlined and repeatable approach has really helped me hone my skills and ensure success in all the roles I have held. Playbook companies are not just great for the sales person, they are also great for customer engagements as it ensures that they get a consistent, efficient and better overall experience, rather than disorganized sales approaches.*

There is no better way to learn than by doing, and oftentimes, progress is more important than perfection, so you can master the craft as you go. In the realm of tech, there are countless opportunities to do just that, because you are in the position to utterly revolutionize the way companies do business. No matter your involvement in it, from a sales, engineering or marketing standpoint, you reach a new level of business acumen as you work in an ever-changing environment. The knowledge you acquire when you are engaged in such an initiative is invaluable and elevates your skillset to new heights.

Tech companies with truly disruptive products and strong innovation have the ability to transform markets, which puts them in an incredibly powerful position. The power of their product and its unique differentiators can lead to it being placed as best in the market and gives multiples of 10x to company valuations.

Organizations like these completely shape the industry around them, not only with the innovation the product delivers, but from their leadership. Top performing software companies will attract not only the best talent, but the best leaders. With that comes high standards of strategies and processes – they look at the science around selling in order to make success repeatable. That is achieved by embracing methodologies and frameworks like MEDDIC, which helps set a new standard for excellence and process discipline.

People that come from these organizations do so with a wealth of knowledge and a track record in executing and delivering success. With a tremendous network of people who have developed and refined their skills to learn from, the potential for your own future is unfathomable. If being at the cutting edge of innovation and disruption sounds intriguing, then tech is for you.

Chapter 1: Why Technology

- With the tech industry's continuous growth and the further explosion of growth and innovation with AI, there has never been a better time to join.

- The innovation innate in tech allows you to work with cutting edge technology and be part of something transformative, unlike anything you've done before.

- The variety within tech means there is something for everyone. You have endless opportunities to grow your career as new companies and roles are created every day, whether it be with a start up or a unicorn.

- The best tech companies invest in their employees' development, giving you numerous learning opportunities that will help you succeed. As you progress in your career, you are constantly being developed and investing in your future and becoming the best you can be.

Chapter Two

WHY SALES?

Sales is an incredible industry to work in; you have the opportunity to learn from incredibly talented individuals, to do interesting work that varies day-to-day, and it can be tremendously rewarding. The perception of sales as a career and the broader understanding of what it can be has shifted significantly – it is now seen as the credible and respected career that it is. The complex and value-driven nature of modern selling has led to B2B sales roles being increasingly viewed as strategic and essential in our contemporary tech industry. This is true not just for companies who are looking to sell their products but for buyers, who expect the people they engage with to be experts in their chosen fields.

Ultimately, it's about working with people and solving problems, so those who are driven and enjoy engaging and communicating with others will thrive. When you join the right sales environment and the right sales culture where the company has a good product, a strong learning and development culture, you will have a real opportunity to grow professionally and personally.

Sales will constantly challenge you; with an ever evolving industry and the competitive atmosphere that comes from working alongside increasingly smart and interesting people, you are pushed to be your best. That being said, it is also hugely rewarding when you hit your targets – not only are you rewarded financially, but you are celebrated with internal kudos from your manager and peers. Part of being a good sales person or leader is rising to that challenge, and when you do, you will see results.

MARINA: *Sales has been incredibly beneficial for my personal and professional growth. Sales offers a unique environment where continuous learning and improvement are integral to success. Each achievement builds momentum, creating a cycle of accomplishment that encourages you to set even higher goals. This dynamic not only enhances your skills but also prepares you for future challenges.*

One of the most valuable aspects of a career in sales is the opportunity it provides to engage with diverse and very senior individuals and organizations. It's crazy to think that at the age of 25 I was presenting business cases to C-Level executives! Interacting with customers and understanding their needs has deepened my insight into various industries and built strong relationships, which are crucial in today's business landscape and even if I were to move out of the industry there are countless learnings I'd take with me.

Additionally, sales requires you to embrace challenges and step out of your comfort zone. For instance, public speaking was once a challenge for me. However, the sales environment pushed me to really face that fear head on, ultimately leading me to present at significant events, including Sales Kickoff gatherings in front of thousands. These experiences have pushed me and expanded my capabilities, opening doors I never imagined.

Overall, a career in sales is much more than pursuing targets;

it's about acquiring valuable skills, building a vast network, and learning how to navigate complex situations effectively. It equips you with tools that are applicable in all areas of life, making it a powerful foundation for future success. I have a quote displayed above my desk that I love: "Success is never owned, it is rented, and the rent is due every day." That is sales.

Each of us took different routes to sales, some more intentional than others, but reflecting on our careers, we identified some essential reasons why we would recommend it to others, especially other women.

PENNY: *A career in sales has given me incredible experiences and financial security – something I'm truly grateful for. I've had the privilege of working alongside brilliant people and sitting across the table from some of the sharpest minds in business, from Private Equity investors to CEOs of FTSE 100 companies. I've negotiated and won multi-million-pound deals, traveled the world, attended world-class sporting events, and, most importantly, helped develop and support the success of those on my teams. The variety, challenge, and opportunity that sales offers is unmatched, and I feel incredibly fortunate to be part of such a dynamic profession.*

LUCY: *I feel so fortunate to have fallen into tech sales at the age of eighteen. This career has not only given me the opportunity to grow personally each year while earning a good salary, but to also travel the world, meet new people and experience so many different things.*

FINANCIAL INDEPENDENCE AND INFLUENCE

While money isn't everything, for any of us considering a career, making money is a factor we take into consideration. In sales, your skills and success will be rewarded. With a good work ethic and the sales talent to match it, it is a career that can be incredibly lucrative.

Sales is largely commission-based – for example, as an Individual Contributor (e.g. an Account Executive), half of your OTE (on-target earnings) rely on commission, and in some places, especially as you get more senior, equity is an additional incentive. That means you get out what you put in. When you work hard and win deals, you are rewarded for it, and it can be life-changing money. These big wins also come with internal recognition – your achievements are celebrated throughout your team.

When you're a top-performing sales professional, you can access other benefits that provide amazing learnings and experiences. That can include traveling the world as you cover new geographies or move to other offices, as well as attending amazing events (which can include all-expenses-paid trips to amazing destinations awarded to top-performers in recognition of all their hard work), travel for meetings, and client entertaining at prestigious sporting, media or networking events. Not only can it allow you to travel the globe, it can also give you the unique opportunity to network within your organization. The very nature of revenue is that it is at the beating heart of growing a company, and therefore connects across all functions. In an informal setting, you can get to know people at more senior levels in ways you otherwise wouldn't get the chance to – it's an occasion to meet and spend time with the best people in the industry, which can be career defining.

Furthermore, when you are a top-performer you get a chance to manage and close some of the biggest and most important deals in the company – which will raise your profile at the senior management level, which can in turn help to establish a great path forward for promotion within the company.

But that isn't all. Unlocking success in sales means unlocking not only a world of opportunities, but financial security, which opens doors to greater opportunities for wealth creation and making your money work for you.

MARINA: *My approach to life has always been grounded in the belief that when unexpected challenges arise – and they inevitably will – I want to have a solid foundation that makes me feel self-sufficient and secure. For me, that foundation was purchasing a home. My journey towards achieving that security motivated me to pursue a career in sales, where I could earn enough to make it a reality. Now that I own my home, I can shift my focus towards other investment opportunities that will benefit both me and my family in the long term.*

Working in sales offers a unique vantage point to observe various businesses and understand the diverse mindsets that drive them. This exposure not only broadens your perspective on earning potential within the industry but also highlights the opportunities to create alternative income streams. The idea of "making money work for you" becomes a tangible goal. With disposable income, I've learned to invest wisely (most of the time), resulting in a deeper understanding of the investments I choose and the companies I can support.

As I transitioned into sales leadership, I discovered a path many take – consulting for startups or becoming seed investors in promising ventures. This financial opportunity was something I hadn't considered when I first entered the sales arena. Now, I love investing in early-stage businesses.

Ultimately, while financial success is important, the real value lies in the opportunities it creates. For me, it's about building businesses and engaging with innovative ideas that truly excite me.

LUCY: *Financial independence is something I have always taken very seriously and strived towards. When I was growing up, I looked around me and started to think about what I wanted to achieve and the reasons why. It was not always about fast cars and big houses, it started with being able to look after myself.*

When I 'fell' into sales at the age of eighteen and found out in the first year, I was pretty good at it, and it paid well, I decided to forgo my space at university to study Sports Science to pursue a career in tech.

I am so grateful I did that, this job has given me a degree of financial freedom I think not everyone has.

PENNY: *During my twenties, I was an Enterprise AE in a US financial services company, and was earning more than a lot of my friends who were in what you would deem 'more respectable careers' at that time. The commission I earned in that time really set me up securely for the future, for which I am very grateful.*

1. VARIETY

In sales, no two days are the same – particularly because there is such variation across roles and the types of work you do within them. Within sales itself the roles include:

DIFFERENT SALES ROLES

Individual Contributor	▎Inside sales ▎Enterprise AE ▎Midmarket AE ▎Account Manager ▎Channel Sales
Leadership	▎Regional/ Geographical Manager ▎Director ▎Regional VP Sales ▎VP Sales ▎VP ▎CRO ▎COO
Supporting Roles	▎SDRs ▎Presales ▎Solution engineer ▎Revenue or Sales operations ▎Enablement

In any role, the work you do differs: from territory planning, to account mapping, to pitching, to pricing, to designing a solution for your customer, to strategic planning, to negotiating, to engaging with senior executives within an organization.

When you're an AE, you are running your own book of business and you are the CEO of that business. You are in charge of your time, your forecast, and your earning potential. As a sales professional, you need to keep in mind that your role is not just about you and your customer, but about bringing in your internal team members to ensure a successful outcome is reached for the customer. Sales is no longer about being the 'lone wolf', it's much more about bringing the right expertise into the sale at the right time. With the support of technical sales consultants, domain experts, SDRs, and CSMs, success comes from close collaboration with your colleagues – whether it's leveraging marketing's content, solution engineers' demos and technical expertise, SDRs' outreach and lead nurturing, or services' domain knowledge. When it comes to any deal or account, there are a lot of moving parts to consider and different hats to wear. Engaging with a number of internal stakeholders injects novelty into your schedule, as no exchange will be like the others. This becomes even more important as you get into leadership. To use a sports metaphor, you're like the coxswain for a rowing team, aligning everyone in pursuit of one goal.

MARINA: *The best sales professionals and leaders I've encountered are those who can inspire their teams to unite around a common goal for the customer. In a landscape where roles across customer success, professional services, and technical teams are measured differently, driving the right alignment and collaboration is an art. When everyone is rowing in the same direction towards achieving a significant goal or outcome for the customer, it not only enhances the overall customer experience but also drives bigger successes. This ability to get the best out of diverse functions under a shared vision is what distinguishes exceptional leaders from the rest.*

Part of the variety that comes with sales is because no two customers are the same. From personality types to challenges faced, no engagement you have with a customer will mirror another. A use-case you attach your solution to in one meeting can be very different to the use-case you share in the next one. The way that you measure success with each customer will vary, just as your messaging may differ based on the ICP (Ideal Customer Profile) and persona. While playbooks ensure consistency in approach, they also define messaging on value tailored to different personas, along with structured methods for selling. You have the license to be creative within this framework. Variety in sales comes not just from engaging with different industries but also from interacting with diverse personas, addressing unique use cases, and adapting to different meeting types depending on where you are in the sales cycle. Some meetings will be focused on presenting, others on discovery, and some on deep dives and technical scoping.

Sales methodologies and best practices continue to evolve – now more than ever with the rise of AI and automation. There is always something new to learn and refine, helping you sharpen your craft and stay at the top of your game.

When you work in a high-growth company, you have an array of opportunities to avoid stagnancy. Revenue is the main driver of organizations, and being in the revenue function means your role has high value. It gives you a seat at the table, and people who do well in revenue tend to be promoted and listened to. It is a great place to kick start your career and is a strong path to promotion, whether it be into sales management or other areas of the revenue business like marketing, pre-sales, customer success, or revenue operations.

Sales isn't 9-5; between time-zones if you work for a global company or travel for meetings, the hours can change day-to-day. It can offer immense flexibility. You don't have to sit at a desk all day – you are out meeting clients and prospects, pitching, making proposals, speaking or networking at public events. Many people we spoke to mentioned travel as a key element as to why they like working in sales. Even in an increasingly remote and online industry, the impact that can be made face-to-face is exponential, and so there are numerous opportunities within sales to visit new countries, whether to meet with customers or internal stakeholders.

If you like working with people, then sales is for you! A defining characteristic of sales and sales leadership is conversation and connecting with people, with your customers as well as with your internal teams. It can involve a lot of networking, but more importantly, it involves a lot of listening; hearing about people's problems and helping to solve them. So much of sales involves relationship building, and the success of those relationships is based on the connections you make and the success you bring to your customers. Sales is most importantly about delivering impact, and forming connections is the most effective way of achieving that.

Through forming connections with your customers, you build Champions – people who have the power and influence to drive your solution forward, a personal investment in its success, and who sell internally on your behalf.

Champions are imperative to a deal's success, as there is nothing more credible than a customer referring you to another person in their network. So, to build them you need to establish a rapport with them as you inform them on your solution.

From engaging with people and building Champions, you can meet and build bonds with a wide range of interesting people who can bring value to you in many ways. If you work in a global role, for example, you can encounter people from different cultures that can offer new insights. In sales, you will never be bored.

2. THINK DIFFERENTLY

Something that can go overlooked about sales is that it is a place where neurodiversity can thrive. Since sales is about problem solving and finding creative ways around issues, people who think a little differently to others stand out because they view problems from a unique angle. While there is no precise data on neurodiversity in the B2B sales workforce specifically, our experience and that of people we have spoken to suggests that many high-performing salespeople may excel because of their ADHD, for example, due to traits such as high energy, hyperfocus, and resilience. Ultimately, as sales is people-centric, it attracts a variety of people who can be very successful.

MARINA: *Sales is fundamentally about creative problem-solving and engaging others, and I believe that neurodiversity can be an advantage. As someone with dyslexia and likely ADHD, I've never excelled in traditional academic settings. While school was often challenging, and my ADHD made it easy to get distracted, I have never viewed these traits as limitations.*

Instead, they have cultivated a sense of resilience and determination in me. I've found that I'm actually more accustomed to working harder than others to achieve similar results, which has ingrained a strong work ethic. In my experience, underdogs often excel in sales precisely because they refuse to give up at the first obstacle. They do the hard things, the things others won't do.

I never expected work to be easy – nothing else in life generally is. This mindset has led me to find unconventional methods to accomplish tasks that others might overlook. I actively seek advice and develop resourcefulness as a result. When written communication is a struggle, I've really worked on my verbal communication skills, both in meetings and networking situations. While I've worked hard to improve my written abilities, I feel most comfortable and effective when engaging face-to-face – which fortunately sales is all about – building Champions and really reading a room.

This strength, I hope translates well into my leadership style. I believe great leadership is about being proactive and inspiring your team, encouraging collaboration and everyone working towards a shared goal. It's not about being confined to your computer; it's about standing up, motivating others, and ensuring that everyone is aligned. Strong interpersonal skills and the ability to lead by example are essential. It's the doers who ultimately make great leaders.

PENNY: *When I was at school my report card always said "Penny would be great if she could just concentrate more!" It wasn't until I was in my forties that I was diagnosed with ADHD (off the back of my son also being diagnosed). On reflection it made sense, I much preferred the client facing work that involved meetings and presenting over and above the heavy administrative tasks. Sales really was the ideal way for me to channel that energy and be successful in the less traditional 'desk job' way.*

3. FAST-PACED

When you work in the constantly growing and innovating world of tech sales, your day-to-day life can be quite fast-paced and high pressure. The nature of having quarterly targets means there is a constant review of how you build pipeline and close opportunities – you need to always be performing. With the industry moving forward and constant advancements made in technology, in order to keep their product current and matching customer expectations and business requirements, or to expand their offering and target market, companies must evolve their product and develop or buy other products and integrations. This opens up new geographies and customer segments for those in sales, because new aspects of the product allow for new problems to solve for customers, while simultaneously requiring the entire team to update their strategies to include the latest techniques and features of the product.

Sales, by its very nature, is quite performance-based. You need to hit your targets consistently to be successful, which creates a kind of pressure that isn't for everyone. There are the highs of making a big win or exceeding your first quarter or full year, and the lows of losing a deal or not getting a call back from a prospect who you were convinced was going to buy from you. It requires not only hard work, but also resilience and an ability to be able to pick yourself up, dust yourself down and move onto the next sale or quarter with gusto.

Markets are consistently competitive, so it's important to stay ahead. Salespeople who are quick on their feet will benefit, because as the customer needs change, you need to be able to meet them at their level. Most customers seeking your solution will be doing so for different reasons, so you need to understand their unique pains and how you can collaborate with them to address it. It's not just about being fast, it's also important to manage your time, to ensure there is time allocated to pipeline building, managing opportunities, continuous learning and administrative tasks. For managers it is similar, but looking at things from a wider team perspective. Your time is your most precious commodity, so it's essential to prioritize activities that deliver the highest value outcomes.

The science of sales, too, is constantly evolving. What customers and investors expect from organizations and from salespeople is often shifting, and there will be an expectation that your sales organization is leveraging the very best of the sales methodologies like MEDDICC, playbooks, technology and AI to stay ahead of the competition.

For AEs and leaders it will be about showing you understand your book of business and making it 'work for you'. It will be about leveraging data to get insights at a granular level on what activities within the sales funnel are yielding the best results, and equally where you are losing deals and what changes can be made to achieve positive results.

Success in sales is about consistency. It is not just about doing well once, but doing it quarter on quarter. Drive and motivation is key to consistent delivery. We will elaborate in Part 2 on the habits of top performing salespeople.

Chapter 2: Why Sales

Sales provides lucrative, commission-based earnings and opportunities for wealth creation, career progression, and networking within the industry.

The fast-paced nature of sales encourages personal growth through challenges, helping individuals improve their skills, build relationships, and adapt to new situations.

The variety within tech means there is something for everyone. You have endless opportunities to grow your career as new companies and roles are created every day, whether it be with a start up or a unicorn.

Sales is a place where neurodiversity can thrive. The very nature of the role makes it a great career choice for those who prefer interacting with people and who excel with a variety of tasks.

HANNAH BATES, MAJORS AE AT DATADOG, ON WHY SHE CHOSE SALES:

> *When I was in university, my degree had a year out in the industry, so I did a placement at IBM. While there, I worked really closely with the sales teams where I had a lot of client interaction, which I found was exactly what worked for me. I applied for the IBM graduate scheme, and never looked back.*

A WORD FROM ALICE CARLISLE, RVP AT WIZ, ON WHY SHE LOVES SALES:

> *Every day, I feel like I'm doing a million different jobs. One minute I'm a project manager, another I'm like a doctor, uncovering someone's pain. I feel incredibly lucky because I make more money than other people who do several years of training and I get to do so many amazing things!*

FLAVIA BROWN, AREA VICE PRESIDENT AT MULTIVERSE, ON WHAT BROUGHT HER TO SALES:

> *I had been in sales for 5 years before moving to tech sales, and I was attracted to it by a few different factors.*
>
> *One: the learning opportunity. I had always had short sales cycles, low value deals and one-call closes, and I had stopped developing and pushing myself, so I wanted to do big enterprise deals worth multi-million pounds.*
>
> *Two: Earning. I knew that people in tech were earning more than I was and I wanted some of that!*
>
> *Three: progression. I was 26 and on a senior leadership team and had very much hit a ceiling. I thought to myself, what am I doing? I'm still young, still hungry and certainly have so much*

more to learn. So I decided to go to a fast-paced, high-growth environment to push myself and progress my career, which I'm glad to say I have done.

Chapter Three

WHY YOU?

So far, we've considered what it is about tech that makes it such an appealing industry to work in, and why working in sales specifically can be an interesting and rewarding career path. But what makes a great salesperson and sales leader? What is it about you that could make you suited to sales, and would allow you to thrive? Think about the following questions:

WHY YOU?
• Do you work well under pressure?
• Are you results-focused?
• Do you love meeting and engaging with people?
• Are you a good communicator and active listener?
• Are you comfortable influencing and negotiating with others?

If you answered yes to these questions, it's likely that sales could be the right career path for you. However, historically there have been some depictions or stereotypes of what a "salesperson" looks like, and how you need to act to be successful in sales. For example, in the 1980s, playwright David Mamet wrote and staged *Glengarry Glen Ross*, a play that centers around four real estate salesmen. In

1992, it was turned into a film starring Al Pacino, Jack Lemmon, and Alec Baldwin. Its main cast is full of recognizable (negative) stereotypes of salespeople; ambitious, deceitful, and border-line slimy, they lie to their customers and cheat one another to get ahead. While the film remains a cult classic, in the modern era, what it says about sales could not be farther from the truth. But people may look at this kind of portrayal of salespeople, and question whether sales is the place for them, if they would actually do well in that industry.

Women, for instance, may look at the male-dominated world of sales, and despite finding a sales role appealing, might not go for it. Research indicates that women are less likely to be confident in applying for roles than their equally qualified male counterparts. A 2019 LinkedIn study found that women are 14% less likely to apply for jobs after viewing them,[13] and a 2024 study from Harvard Business School found that 6 percent of qualified women applied for a job classified as "expert", compared to 22 percent of qualified men.[14]

However, if you look at the data, women have the capability to not only succeed in sales but to become the top performers. It has been found that women in sales have 11% higher win rates than their male counterparts.[15] In addition, evidence shows that female-owned start-ups produce more than twice the revenue of male-owned start-ups (even though, more often than not, women receive less investment).[16] As Adam Quartermaine, SVP of EMEA at Harness, formerly of Sprinklr, told us, "If you look at the top 20% at Sprinklr, they're all female."

ATTRIBUTES OF A GREAT SALESPERSON AND SALES LEADER

Someone may have a perception of what makes a good salesperson, and think that they share none of those traits. You could lose out on an amazing opportunity or promotion because you are unaware that you have qualities that could make you a seriously successful salesperson or leader. None of the attributes that make a person good at sales are exclusive to one gender. An interesting observation that we have uncovered is that a lot of the aspects that make someone good at sales are found to be stronger in women! These female superpowers can give women an advantage in sales and leadership, making them exceptional at connecting with those around them and driving success.

1. HIGH EQ

In our experience, women are likely to have a high level of emotional intelligence. This is supported by the fact that women are well-equipped to recognize non-verbal emotional cues; a 2014 study compiled research on abilities to read things like facial expressions, body posture, and tone of voice, and deduced that women tended to perform highly.[17] When you have high emotional intelligence, it allows you to read a room, and assess how your customers or colleagues could be feeling. You can tell when they're interested, or when they're frustrated. The best sellers are emotionally intelligent for a number of reasons; one example being they can perceive when they have touched on a powerful pain point by the customer's reaction. With EQ, you can see if someone is engaged with you, and if not, that can determine who might not be convinced by your solution, or who might be outright against it. You can then pivot your approach to align with what they would prefer.

LUCY: *Success in tech sales isn't just about what you sell – it's about how well you understand people. Emotional intelligence (EQ) is the key to building trust, navigating complex deals, and creating lasting customer relationships. I believe women often excel in this space as we lead with empathy, listen deeply and adapt with agility. In a world where connections drive conversations, EQ isn't just a soft skill – it's a competitive advantage.*

MARINA: *Personally, I believe women tend to be much better at reading a room. Throughout my sales career, I've found that my empathy allows me to connect with others on a deeper level. Women often have a unique ability to mirror the emotions and perspectives of those around us. We can intuitively gauge someone's personality and are mindful of giving them space to express themselves. Rather than overpowering or speaking over others, we prioritize allowing their voices to be heard, fostering an environment that encourages open dialogue and collaboration. This sensitivity not only enhances our interactions but also strengthens relationships, making us effective communicators and collaborators in sales.*

2.   RESILIENCE

As a salesperson, you encounter challenges constantly, and resilience is what enables you to handle bad news in a constructive and effective way. Managing expectations with prospects, customers, and managers requires a steady mindset, and as a sales leader, this becomes even more critical – every escalation will land on your desk. You will ultimately be responsible for meeting quarterly targets, ensuring your team stays on track, and managing difficult customer situations. Research has found that in a crisis, female leaders are incredibly effective, in part due to their resilience in high-pressure situations.[18]

Resilient individuals excel in crisis management not just because they respond well to problems, but because they anticipate and mitigate them before they escalate. Recognizing potential obstacles early prevents major disruptions and keeps momentum strong. Leveraging data and tracking key indicators can help prevent crises, such as missing revenue targets, before they become insurmountable. Ultimately, those who thrive under pressure are resilient – they remain steady, honest, and focused on solutions, always prioritizing the customer's needs while navigating challenges with confidence.

MARINA: *When I sense something going off track, I have an inherent bias for taking immediate action to address the issue. I believe in acting swiftly because I genuinely care about outcomes. My overarching philosophy – particularly in sales – is that making quick decisions is crucial, especially when navigating time-sensitive situations. I've always championed the importance of uncovering bad news early; this practice allows us more time to respond and devise solutions. By identifying potential issues long before they escalate into crises, we can proactively prevent problems altogether. That's why I strive to foster a culture where we celebrate transparency and the sharing of bad news, as this ultimately leads to stronger collaboration and success.*

3.   COMMUNICATION

In sales, particularly enterprise sales, you are looking for long-term strategic partnerships. To succeed as an AE, you need to find people who are invested in your deal and have the motivation and ability to drive its success forward internally. To do that, you need to make connections, and communication is the best way to do that. Salespeople who are able to communicate effectively with customers can build trust with them, and customers are more likely to buy from people they trust. That means talking to prospective customers using language that resonates with them, with a compelling message that directly relates to their pain point.

For a team to be successful, they need to know the common goal that they are working towards and their role in it. So as a sales leader, consistent and clear communication is essential to driving the team forward to that common goal. They cannot win alone, and it is the sales leader's responsibility to collaborate with other teams across the organization to clearly communicate what is needed for everyone to win. Leaders who communicate clearly and consistently on team and individual purpose and expectations, will be able to understand and explain how the teams can work together to make those wins happen, as everyone will know what is expected of them and what the leader will do for them.

MARINA: *When I assess my sales team, I notice that those who excel are the ones capable of distilling complex problems into straightforward solutions. Customers tend to feel more at ease when they're working with someone who has encountered similar issues numerous times and is genuinely committed to helping them resolve their challenges. This ability hinges on clear communication. If you enter a sales cycle and add unnecessary complexity, it can create the perception that the solution is daunting, causing customers to hesitate or shy away from engagement. Keeping things simple not only builds trust but also fosters a collaborative environment where customers feel supported and empowered to move forward.*

LUCY: *Communication is key in all we do, whether that's with internal teams in setting clear goals and objectives, or with a customer in building trust and rapport from the get-go, both* *are important. Effective communication in sales includes active listening, concise messaging and most importantly, customization. No two customers or people are the same, and you have to change the way you communicate and interact specifically to that person. I find women, due to the aforementioned EQ, often have stronger communication skills.*

PENNY: *As a leader, clear and consistent communication is key. People in the business want to know what is expected of them, what the measure of success is,, and what support they will get from their manager and the business to ensure their success. I also think regular, open and transparent communication is important. I have a cadence of weekly leadership team meetings where we openly discuss key topics and solutions, and quarterly 'All Hands' with the wider organization where I am open about the financial data, our performance, and also provide a place to celebrate people and successes as well as Q&A.*

4. ACTIVE LISTENING

Sales is about solving problems – and to solve problems, you need to understand them. That is why a salesperson who listens to their customers with intent will succeed. While it isn't a gender-specific trait, women are often considered to be better at active listening due to a combination of psychological and social factors, which enables them to be great salespeople.

For example, since women typically score higher in EQ, they are more likely to pick up on tone, facial expressions, and emotions when someone is speaking, leading to deeper listening. Additionally women tend to use more eye contact, nodding, and verbal affirmations to show they are engaged. This encourages the speaker to share more and fosters better communication.

MARINA: *There is no bigger compliment from a customer or prospect when they say, 'Thank you. I think you understand my business and its challenges better than some of our employees.'*

5.   EMPATHY

Researchers credit women with qualities like heightened interpersonal sensitivity, attentiveness to others' needs and motivations, and a tendency to favor open, balanced, and collaborative relationships.[19] That is to say, women are often quite empathetic. Empathy is often overlooked in sales and sales leadership, but it is one of the most powerful differentiators between a good leader and a great one. An empathetic sales professional prioritizes the customer's needs, taking the time to understand their challenges and goals. This approach fosters trust and long-term relationships, making it easier to tailor the experience to the customer.

From a leadership standpoint, empathy is about truly caring for your team – their well-being, development, and success. An empathetic leader doesn't just focus on results; they invest in their people, ensuring they feel valued and supported. This doesn't mean avoiding accountability or lowering expectations – on the contrary, when the team knows their leader genuinely cares, they are more engaged, motivated, and driven to perform at their best. Studies have shown that empathy in leadership is pivotal not only in driving team performance and engagement, but in reducing employee burnout and improving retention.[20] By leading with empathy, you cultivate trust, enhance team performance, and create a work environment where people feel valued and empowered to succeed.

PENNY: *Anyone can be a manager if they have people reporting to them. But true leadership isn't about titles – it's about trust.*

Your team may follow your directions because they have to, but they'll only be inspired to go the extra mile when they know you have their back, that you genuinely care about them, and that their success matters to you as much as your own.

6.   DRIVE

Some of the skills that make a great salesperson can be learned, but one thing that will set you above the rest is the drive to succeed. Sales is all about discipline and resilience, and that comes from your drive. When you are eager to get up every morning and do it all again, that is what will make you the best salesperson you can be; it's about showing up every day. The resilience that comes with being driven means treating no as a great opportunity to problem solve and figure out how to get that yes. If you give up easily, you're probably not going to be as good as your peers. Drive is necessary to push you to constantly learn and improve, whether you're an individual contributor or a leader. Investing time in continuous learning and improvement is so important, and you need to have the motivation to do it.

LUCY: *Tech sales isn't for the faint of heart – it demands resilience, drive and an unshakeable belief in yourself. As women, we often have to push harder, prove ourselves more, and break through barriers that shouldn't exist. But grit sets the best apart. It's the fuel that keeps us going after every setback, the determination to hit every target, and the courage to claim our place at the top. In this industry talent opens the door- but drive is what keeps it open. When I'm in, I'm 100% in.*

PENNY: *I think people can forget the importance of consistent hard work. I have put so many long hours in to get to where I am. I worked weekends, I have flown back from holidays for* *important pitches. I have made sure I am always there for my customers, and have worked hard to remain one step ahead of the competition with lots of preparation and constant learning. I think my willingness to always be there for my customers ensured I developed real customer loyalty, and their advocacy has really driven more new business for me and helped that success.*

When it comes to female-specific qualities that can make us great salespeople and sales leaders, we need to remember that it takes resilience to be a woman in sales. While we wish it wasn't the case, there are obstacles that we have to overcome that our male peers just don't; from unconscious bias to everyday sexism. What it means, though, is that female salespeople are tough. When deals look like they're going to be unsuccessful, we can push through, because if we listened to the first 'no', we would have given up long ago. Equally, when we do hear that 'no', we can bounce back without letting it get to us.

People take a lot of different paths to sales and leadership, and they are attracted to it for different reasons. We hope that the perspectives we've shared resonate with you and inspire you to consider software sales as a possible career path.

IN THE WORDS OF MELISSA DI DONATO, CEO AND CHAIR AT KYRIBA:

I think that we as women have an innate capability to communicate and have empathy towards the people that we're working with and selling to. We seek to understand, we don't push. Not to speak negatively about anyone, but when it comes to what makes women different, it's that they have empathy, which impacts the way we go through the sales process. The ability to listen deeply and solve problems is innate in who we are, and those are very strong characteristics in enterprise selling.

MARINA: *Sales lies in navigating the ups and downs, embracing both the challenging days and the victorious ones. I always encourage my team to celebrate bad news, as it helps us maintain a positive outlook and prevents us from becoming discouraged during tougher times. By fostering this mindset, we can sustain our motivation and resilience, ensuring that we remain focused and driven, regardless of the circumstances. This approach not only bolsters individual morale but also strengthens our overall team dynamics.*

A WORD FROM FRANCESCA BOWEN, GLOBAL VP, CLOUD GTM AT DARKTRACE:

Before I moved into tech sales, I was working in International Relations and Politics, and I was struggling financially. As part of my professional development, I had a mentor who was a female leader in tech. She talked about the need for more women in tech, and seeing her success really appealed to me, so I worked my way up!

THE NEED FOR FEMALE SALES LEADERS

One of the challenges women in sales face is the lack of female role models in leadership. When women don't see others like them at the top, it can feel like those roles are out of reach. Strong role models don't just set the standard for what women can achieve – they also reinforce the respect women deserve in leadership. Without that representation, it's easy to feel discouraged. And unfortunately, this creates a cycle: if fewer women pursue leadership roles, there are fewer role models for the next generation, making it even harder to change the status quo.

It is in the interest of organizations to have women in leadership positions; it has been found that female-led teams have 3% better quota attainment rates than male-led teams, for example.[21] A study by BI Norwegian Business School concluded that women are well-suited to leadership, because they tend to possess many of the key attributes of a successful leader, including emotional stability, and an openness to new experiences.[22]

Much of what makes someone a skilled seller, like empathy and good communication, will equally make them strong sales leaders. Women's inclination towards the collective interests of the group (having a 'team-first' approach) and attentiveness to others situates them well for leadership. Since women are typically caregivers, they can nurture their team and guide them to be the best versions of themselves, without being overbearing or harsh.

Attention to detail, for example, is a trait associated with women, though not something only women have. It is a crucial skill needed for success, as salespeople need to carefully analyze customer needs, track engagement, and tailor solutions to each client. Women's ability to notice small, but important details, such as a prospect's pain, buying signals, or subtle shifts in conversations, can give them an edge to building strong relationships and closing deals. Additionally, attention to detail is key in managing large and complex deal cycles, ensuring accurate proposals, and following up effectively. This precision helps maintain credibility, reduce mistakes, and drive higher sales success. As a leader, it means you may catch things that those in your team do not, and you can correct their course, or further propel their success.

LUCY: *Some of the best sales people I have worked with are women. Their ability to build champions, ensure consistent and high quality engagements at each step of the sales cycle and the ability to handle difficult negotiations by reading the room is amazing to watch.*

ANNIE ANONYMOUS*: I have a diverse team, and I can confidently say that the women on my team have far better attention to detail than the men. The number of changes and iterations we have to do in a review of a document when working with the female sellers is 70% less than the males. I had one example of a tenured seller who in one presentation needed over 45 changes made, even though they felt it was 'ready to present'. Is this laziness or lack of caring because they believe that it's not important or just simply they are lacking in the trait?*

A 2007 study identified four general categories into which leadership skills could be grouped, of which interpersonal skills were identified as the second most significant skill category when it came to successful leadership, outweighing both business and strategic skills.[23] Interpersonal skills, we have seen, are a strength found often in women. Therefore, they are positioned well for leadership roles.

Women in leadership genuinely care about their team, which from the start means all decisions made are for the benefit of the team. This approach leads to the betterment of the team as it demonstrates a willingness to have their back, and so builds trust.

An important aspect of leadership is creating an environment where it is safe for them to fail. If someone isn't afraid of failure, it means they are more willing to take risks – and that is how they grow. A key element of building a high performance team is giving them opportunities to take risks, learn, and become better. Women's openness to new experiences means that they are open to new learning opportunities; and when you recognize that there is always a chance to learn, for yourself and for your team, that is how you become a strong leader.

It's essential that we have more leaders who are empathetic, who are strong communicators, and who center their teams, and so looking for people who have these qualities, regardless of gender, is how we can find greater success.

PENNY: *For me great leadership starts with genuinely caring about your team and wanting to see them succeed. One of the most fulfilling parts of leadership is helping people grow – whether that's through direct coaching, recommending mentors and training, or connecting them with others in the sales community.*

There's nothing more rewarding than watching someone you've supported go on to become a great leader themselves.

MARINA: *Creating a place where people feel safe to fail is top of my list in everything I do – ultimately it paves the way for growth which is what all top performers are constantly seeking out. I dedicate significant effort to ensure that I build trust with my teams so I can get the best out of them. From a leadership perspective, this involves being present for my team and actively removing roadblocks that hinder their progress and always being there to listen.*

One particular rep who joined my team exemplifies that. While she was always a solid performer, she struggled with confidence and never reached the top tier. Together, we worked loads on her development, tackling a major deal together – the largest of her career. Interestingly, it was also the biggest deal I had closed, although I kept that to myself at the time. Now, I watch her confidently stand in front of 200 people, sharing her experience and the value she delivered to the customer – articulating what she learned and how she achieved it. Witnessing her transformation into someone who is unconsciously competent in her abilities is truly rewarding. It's the best feeling in the world to see someone thrive as a result of the guidance and support provided, and it reinforces the importance of what you are doing and the genuine impact you can have on people's lives – both in and outside of work.

LUCY: *While I don't think there's one way to be a good leader, a trait that makes a strong leader is empathy. Empathy is the secret weapon in tech sales leadership – it's not a nice to have, it's a superpower. It's what builds high performing teams, creates a culture of trust, and turns managers into true leaders. Women often bring a natural ability to listen, support and inspire, helping teams navigate challenges, and reach new heights. Not only being there when they are winning and celebrating the success, but being there when they are losing and working out how to turn it around, while learning from the mistakes made. When people feel understood and valued, they don't just work harder, they grow, thrive, and succeed together. And that's how you build a winning team.*

IS LEADERSHIP THE RIGHT PATH FOR YOU?

As we've talked about, each of us has taken a different path to leadership, and for none of us was it an easy decision. However, leadership is one of the most rewarding steps you can take in your career; there is nothing quite like taking the expertise you have gained and passing it on, and watching others succeed because of your knowledge. These are some questions that you can consider:

IS LEADERSHIP THE RIGHT PATH FOR YOU?

- **Do you want to create a common vision and inspire people through it?**

- **Do you enjoy mentoring and leading people to succeed?** *(as a leader you will need to guide and support a team in the tough times without leaning on them)*

- **Do you have a strong track record in sales yourself?** *(Credibility as a leader comes with a track record)*

- **Are you comfortable creating and executing on strategies?**

- **Can you balance empathy and authority?**

LUCY: *Before there were vaccinations available, I got incredibly sick with COVID, and I thought I was going to die. I was lying in bed and I thought, "If I die, all I'm going to be known for is that I was a really good sales person."*

In my career, I've been fortunate to learn from some really great people who have taught me amazing things, and in that moment I realized that I wanted to pay that forward. I thought, if I could show other people who want to do really well in sales what I've learned, I could pass that knowledge down, and that would be a really good thing to do.

So, when I got better I told my leader at the time that I wanted to take that step. When a role came up in the team, I went through the internal process and was successfully promoted into my first Enterprise Leadership role.

It's been really gratifying in the four years since I took that role to see my team embracing the knowledge I've shared with them and succeeding too. For example, there are some people who I took on in the beginning who were good but never hit their number, and who now overachieve consistently. Obviously there is still development needed, but it's wonderful to see someone take what you have taught them and flourish and do well. It makes me really proud.

Making the move into leadership is a decision to be made with foresight and informed of all the facts. Making that step isn't for everyone, and there is no set time as to when you should do it. Everyone works at their own pace and only you will know when the time is right. Someone could be an amazing IC, but it might not guarantee that they'd be an effective sales leader. The rewards of leadership come with new responsibilities; no longer is your focus on your deals and the money you take home, but on your team's successes. You might not be as independent as you were before, because you are guiding and leading your team.

To master leadership, you need to tackle certain challenges; team members operate at different paces and with different motivations compared to what their leader might be familiar with, so you need to be prepared for some trial and error when it comes to managing a team.

MARINA: *When I was first approached about stepping into a leadership role, I was genuinely surprised and definitely did not think I was ready. I initially resisted, feeling unprepared and prioritizing my financial stability. I had a deep love for my customers and was delivering significant value as a rep, achieving back-to-back million-dollar quarters for the company and having a huge amount of fun – controlling my own calendar and really putting my all into my business.*

For me, it was the opportunity to build a legacy that ultimately persuaded me to embrace it. For me, legacy means creating a network of people who trust and respect you, fostering relationships that open doors to various experiences. I think of Dali Rajic, for whom I worked for about seven years; when he joined Zscaler, I followed him without hesitation. I didn't know much about the company, but I trusted Dali as a fantastic leader who had made brilliant previous decisions and cared hugely about the people that had worked for him.

Moreover, I recognized that opportunities like running a significant book of business don't come around often and sometimes even if the timing isn't quite as planned you need to take risks and make jumps that feel uncomfortable. The Annual Recurring Revenue (ARR) I managed at Zscaler resembles that of a pre-IPO startup – and now that experience stands me in great stead for future opportunities – I hope.

Leadership also offers unique perks. In sales as a rep, earnings can fluctuate wildly, making it challenging to achieve financial balance. However, as a leader, you become an integral part of the company's success, with a large proportion of your comp often being in stock – I always see this as an investment that provides an additional revenue stream and a constant flow of the team's deals can provide a more stable income. This shift in perspective allows you to make decisions that benefit not just yourself but the organization as a whole and it ignites an even greater energy to provide a meaningful impact on the company's trajectory.

LUCY: *I took 21 years to decide to take the step into leadership, and every day I now think, "Why did I not do this sooner?" Ahead of taking that step, I was worried about the extra responsibility that it would bring, about the fact that I would be responsible for other people's forecasts to the business, and how they perform. I also had doubts as to whether I would be as good as my counterparts. In the early days of leading the team I would try and mimic their styles, which did not work well for me.*

Moving into leadership has given me so much more than I ever imagined. It is not an easy transition, but the rewards far outweigh it. There is nothing I love more than seeing my team achieve and develop, week on week and year on year. The role challenges me daily, but I love the fact I have the ability to learn and grow myself also, and impact wider company decisions and results.

One thing I learned early on: to be a good leader you need to be yourself, embrace what you do and be confident in your abilities- you would not be in the position if others did not believe in you and your capabilities – so use this to thrive.

PENNY: *Leadership wasn't something I initially wanted to do. I was an IC (individual contributor) for 15 years and enjoyed the freedom with my time and the high earnings that came from the* *commission in winning big deals. However my team and I went through a succession of not very good managers and I started to get frustrated. I had also reached the point where I wanted to have an input in strategy and contribute to the company's success outside of my day-to-day sales.*

Like Marina, I was initially hesitant about becoming a manager – I think part of that was that I wasn't sure I would be any good at it, and part of it was the idea of leaving a job where I was in complete control of my number and my destiny, to a job where I had to find a way to get everyone to their number was daunting.

I am glad to say that I loved moving into leadership, and continue to find it rewarding. It can be hard, and I continue to learn a lot about myself (both good and bad). I was lucky as my company gave me management training, which has proven to be invaluable. It helped me understand the kind of leader I needed to be, and the skills I needed to develop. Being a good sales person does not always equal a good sales leader, yet so few companies invest in training their front line managers. I continue to place a lot of importance in investing in my management teams, as well as myself.

WHY AREN'T THERE MORE FEMALE SALES LEADERS?

Being a woman in leadership, particularly in sales leadership, has evolved over the years. In the 1980s, women held only 23% of all professional selling jobs, and sales leadership was essentially out of the question.[24] Fortunately, as time has progressed, we can see the percentages of women in C-suite and executive positions trending upwards.

In 1995, only 2.4% of those leading Fortune 500 companies were women.[25] By 2004, this number had risen to 28.8%, and again in 2018 to 38.6%.[26]

| PERCENTAGE OF WOMEN LEADING FORTUNE 500 COMPANIES

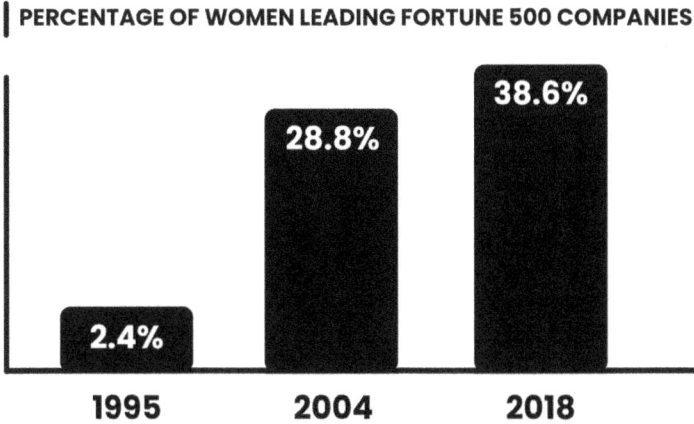

2.4%	**28.8%**	**38.6%**
1995	**2004**	**2018**

In 2015, a McKinsey study found that women accounted for an average of 16% of executive teams in the US and 12% in the UK.[27]

**| PERCENTAGE OF WOMEN IN EXECUTIVE TEAMS
IN 2015**

16%	12%
US	**UK**

As of 2024, 34% of VPs and 29% of C-suite leaders are women – that's a 12% increase at the C–suite level since 2015.[28]

PERCENTAGE OF WOMEN AT VP AND C-SUITE LEVEL

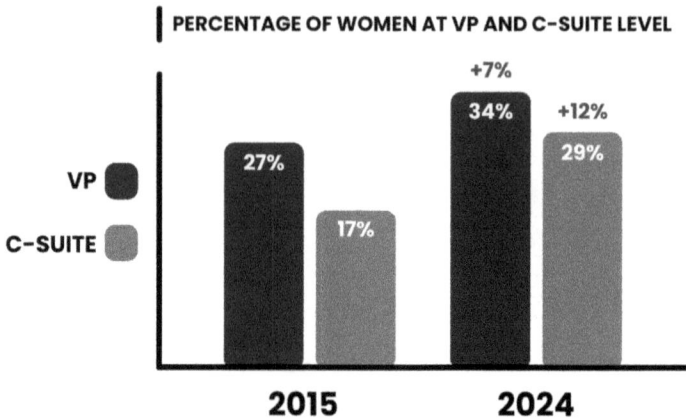

Slowly, but steadily, we are making our presence known among leadership teams. But there is still a long way to go. When we look specifically at tech sales, the disparity between men and women is still quite distinct – in 2021, only 28.8% software sales representatives in the US were women.[29]

When you consider the fact that women make up 48% of entry level positions in the corporate pipeline, it becomes clear that something is missing. We are seeing more women in leadership positions than ever before, but it is still not enough. 39% of corporate managers are women, a number that decreases by 2% at the director level.[30] This rate of decrease continues as you look further up the corporate ladder, with the above mentioned 34% of VPs being women, followed by 29% of SVPs.[31]

Part of the reason for the lack of female sales leaders comes down to numbers. If you don't have more women entering the funnel, it is harder to promote women further up the ladder.

LUCY: *If we want to have more women in leadership, we need* to start by hiring more women at the ground level. The pipeline matters. When we create opportunities for female talent to enter tech sales, grow and thrive in a safe environment, we are not just filling roles, we are building the next generation of leaders. Diversity at the top starts with inclusion at the bottom.

ANNIE ANONYMOUS: *I sit in leadership meetings with the recruitment teams and the male leaders getting so excited that "they hired one," meaning a woman.*

I find this so offensive, and for people to get praise for hiring a woman is so backwards. When I speak up, I get knocked down, with excuses of "I didn't mean it like that."

This mindset needs to change.

But the funnel is only half the story. When you look at the percentages of women in leadership in software technology, it becomes clear that something else is happening:[32]

| PERCENTAGE OF WOMEN IN SOFTWARE IN 2023

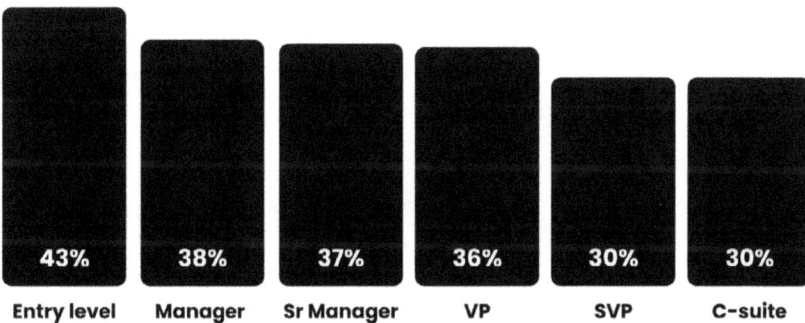

Entry level	Manager	Sr Manager	VP	SVP	C-suite
43%	38%	37%	36%	30%	30%

A study by McKinsey found that women are not getting promoted at the same rate as their male peers; in 2024, for every 100 men who are promoted from entry-level to manager, only 81 women were promoted.[33] As you probably can guess, it isn't because women aren't as ambitious as their male colleagues – studies have shown they are equally so.[34]. Nor is it that they aren't as good, or don't work as hard as their male colleagues.

It's not just that women aren't being promoted at the same rate as men, they are also leaving their companies before they get to the C-suite; "for every woman at the director level who gets promoted to the next level, two women directors are choosing to leave their company."[35] While there has been a rise in opportunities for women in senior positions to network and coach within the female C-suite community, there is still a significant shortage of women when you go higher up the ladder.

PENNY: *We need to talk about why fewer women are making it into senior leadership, or leaving before they get to leadership. Obviously, there are a number of reasons, but we can't ignore that there is a drop off around the time women have a family. It's not the only reason of course, but there is a correlation. For some they may be on maternity leave when a promotion is available, or for others they simply cannot afford to come back to work due to the balance of childcare cost and lack of flexibility.*

In their 2023 Women in the Workplace study, McKinsey refer to this as the "broken rung" in the corporate ladder.[36] But what causes it?

It isn't that women aren't asking to be promoted – McKinsey found that they ask for promotions as often as their male colleagues do.[37] What has been found is that women are promoted less often due to "performance bias" – as a generalization, they are hired and promoted based on what they have already achieved, while men are hired and promoted based on what they could achieve in the future.[38] This tends to disadvantage women who may not have the same kinds of track records as their peers.

PENNY: *I once worked for a fantastic female sales leader – one of the few women on an otherwise male-dominated leadership team.*

Over the course of a year, I watched as she was systematically maneuvered out by a male counterpart who saw her as a threat because she held the role he wanted.

There was a clear undercurrent of a boys' club within the leadership team. They played golf together, shared the same jokes, and went out drinking – he was part of it, and she wasn't. When it came time for the promotion, he got the CRO role, and she was pushed out.

Combined with other factors, the broken rung means there isn't enough diversity at the leadership level, which can cause an organization to really lose out. There are ways that organizations can overcome this broken rung, which will be covered in a later section. When women are in sales leadership positions, as we have seen, they can have a tremendous impact. n are in sales leadership positions, as we have seen, they can have a tremendous impact.

It is more important than ever to highlight that women pursuing careers in sales have a path to the top – if it is something that you want, it is achievable, and somewhere you could thrive.

ANNIE ANONYMOUS: *Being a CRO is not something everyone wants. Some say it's one of the toughest jobs on the Exec team. It really depends on the culture of the company and Exec team, but the reality is, CROs have one of the shortest tenures in leadership – on average, just 18 months. They're often the first to go if the numbers aren't there, even though growth is rarely down to one person; it's a combination of factors.*

It can also be a lonely role - you're the only one responsible for 'winning' revenue, and when targets are missed, those hard conversations fall squarely on your shoulders. Sales is usually the first function to face scrutiny from investors and CEOs, and unlike product or finance, it doesn't always command the same level of respect at the Exec table. It's a high-stakes role – when things are going well, it's great, but when they're not, the pressure is relentless.

It takes a certain kind of person to handle the constant expectation of delivering quarterly and annual revenue targets, knowing that every decision is under a microscope. You have to be tough, because there will always be difficult conversations, and being the only female CRO in an all-male Exec team only adds another layer of challenge.

The definition of what it means to be a salesperson is evolving; it is no longer so clear what box they fit into. After all, sales is no longer a realm dominated by one gender. As a result, what it means to be a sales leader is becoming even more nebulous. As we cross the transforming landscape that sales has become, women are proving themselves to be not just participants but groundbreakers. The insights shared throughout this chapter reinforce the vital importance and impact women bring to sales. They are not merely survivors, but conquerors. Women's distinct strengths, as we have discussed, uniquely equip them for sales and leadership excellence.

As more women enter the realm of tech sales, its future looks set to be not just inclusive and diverse, but teeming with potential, bursting with innovation, and paving the way for the leaders of tomorrow.

Chapter 3: Why You

Emotional intelligence, communication, empathy, resilience, and drive are essential for building trust, solving problems, and leading teams effectively; these traits often align with strengths found in women.

A lack of female role models in sales leadership can discourage women from aspiring to such roles. Visibility of successful female leaders inspires confidence and sets a standard for what women can achieve in sales. Organizations benefit from diverse leadership, as female-led teams often outperform male-led teams.

Great leaders prioritize their team's success by fostering trust, removing roadblocks, and offering mentorship. Building an environment where failure is safe encourages innovation, resilience, and long-term growth for both individuals and teams.

PART TWO

HOW TO HAVE A *LONG AND SUCCESSFUL CAREER* IN TECH SALES

Your career in sales and leadership is shaped by the steps you take and the strategies you implement. From preparing for your first interview to thriving in senior leadership, this chapter provides practical guidance to help you stand out, succeed, and grow with confidence. You'll gain insights into building a compelling personal brand, mastering the interview process, and assessing potential employers to ensure they align with your values and long-term aspirations.

We map the journey from SDR to the C-suite, outlining the key responsibilities at each stage and sharing real-life stories of what works – and what doesn't. You'll learn best practices from those who have successfully navigated the path before you. Think of this as both a guide and a roadmap, designed to help you advance in your career with clarity, purpose, and strategic intent.

While sales is a field full of opportunities, women often face additional hurdles along the way. Unconscious biases, exclusion, and confidence barriers can create obstacles that, while not unique to women, tend to be more prevalent and persistent. This chapter sheds light on these challenges through personal stories and actionable advice, equipping you with strategies to overcome them. By understanding these dynamics and developing approaches to navigate them, you'll not only build a successful career for yourself but also contribute to creating a more inclusive and equitable workplace.

Success in sales isn't just about closing deals – it's about mastering key career-defining conversations. Whether you're negotiating a pay raise, advocating for a promotion, or discussing parental leave, how you approach these conversations can have a lasting impact. We'll explore proven techniques to help you navigate these moments with confidence and professionalism

Finally, no career is built in isolation. Mentors, coaches, and champions can play a transformative role in your growth, opening doors, offering guidance, and pushing you to reach your full potential. This section provides insights on how to cultivate meaningful relationships with the right people, ensuring you have the support, feedback, and advocacy needed to accelerate your career.

By the end, you'll have a clear blueprint for navigating your sales career with confidence and purpose. With the right strategies, tools, and mindset, you'll be ready to take action – overcoming challenges, seizing opportunities, and shaping a career that aligns with your ambitions.

Chapter Four

LANDING THE ROLE

Embarking on a career in tech sales is unlike any other. It's a role where you will encounter a rich variety of people and be presented with an opportunity to have access to different parts of the business and to progress. We talked in Part One about the variety that sales offers as a profession. Much like running your own business, in sales you are responsible for managing your most important commodity – your time, and maniacally prioritizing activity to ensure you hit your targets. It involves many skill sets, from developing customer pitches and relationships, to building pipeline and managing your forecast. It can be hard work, but it can be interesting and impactful. But before you do so, you need to know where to begin.

As we touched on previously, there is no specific route to tech sales. We spoke to a number of professionals across the industry; some people came to it straight from school, others from university. Some people were working in other industries and were encouraged to pursue a career in tech by a mentor, career coach or even a client. The beauty about sales is that it is open to all. Your journey will likely differ from ours, which is part of what makes sales so great – no matter where you begin, you can thrive in your sales journey.

Whether you're looking to enter a new company, or seeking a new role in your current organization, preparation is key. There might be concerns about lack of experience, particularly if this is your first time stepping into a certain role, so it will be important to highlight key skills. For example, first time managers will need to have examples of leading key projects or initiatives, examples of mentorship, as well as key attributes like good communication, strong being methodical and process driven. If you do not have these skills, then you will need to develop them before applying for the role. You can align yourself with top performers who you can learn from and put in the effort to learn habits and traits that make people in those roles successful. If you want to set yourself apart, you need to put in time and thought into your preparation.

CREATING YOUR PERSONAL BRAND

When it comes to getting ahead in sales, you can never underestimate the power of branding. A strong personal brand in B2B sales is essential for building credibility and attracting new customers, and helps people get a feel for who you are and what you stand for. Your personal brand is defined by how you present yourself at all levels – from your LinkedIn profile and posts to your resume, to panels or podcasts you join or events you attend. An element of your personal branding is your physical presentation. While it may seem obvious, dressing professionally is often overlooked, and neglecting this aspect can leave a lasting negative impression – this can be a very sensitive topic as well. The way you present yourself – whether in the office, during a Zoom meeting, or on LinkedIn – sets the tone for how others perceive you. So why not curate an image that conveys professionalism and commands respect? By doing so, you establish the expectations for how you want to be seen in the eyes of your customers or your colleagues.

Below are the key steps to consider when building your personal brand.

PENNY: *Building your brand and voice in your industry is so important, but I'll admit – it didn't come naturally to me at first, and is something I am still working on. A few years ago, I made a conscious decision to put myself out there to elevate my profile and open up new career opportunities. It felt uncomfortable at the start. I wasn't a big social media user, and sharing my thoughts publicly was outside my comfort zone. But I set a goal for myself: once a quarter, I'd contribute to a podcast, join a panel, take a speaker slot, or write a post. What I didn't expect was how well it would be received. People have engaged and new opportunities have come my way. In fact, this book wouldn't even exist if I hadn't done a panel with Lucy and Marina! So if you're unsure about putting yourself out there, take the first step. You never know what doors it will open, as well as help you attract new talent into your teams.*

LUCY: *Your personal brand in tech sales is more than just your results – it's your reputation, your voice, and the value you bring beyond the numbers. My advice here, and what I have been trying to do over the past 5 years, is to elevate it. You can do this by being the go-to expert, building authentic relationships, and consistently showing up with confidence, knowledge and integrity. In the tech industry, the best salespeople are not just sellers, they are trusted advisors, thought-leaders and problem solvers... who are likeable.*

LEVERAGING LINKEDIN

LinkedIn is the clear starting point to establish your personal brand in a professional setting in a way that communicates to prospective employers and colleagues who you are. It acts like a constant resume, displaying your achievements and career progression in real time.

Here are some top tips for curating your LinkedIn profile to clarify your personal brand:

FIVE KEY STEPS TO BUILDING YOUR PERSONAL BRAND:

- **Define your value proposition: establish what makes you unique** (*skills, expertise, problems you can solve*).

- **Set your tone** (*consistent, authentic, polite and professional*).

- **Content creation: develop a point of view. Present insights relevant to your industry and area of expertise.**

- **Build your network: connect with other thought leaders, attend key events, and get references for your profile.**

- **Amplify your voice: guest on podcasts, write blogs, attend speaking events.**

Credentials, Skills and Experience

- Include references from customers and employees (past and present) to illustrate your character and capabilities.
- Be sure to list any awards or extra courses you have done related to your field – it's a great way to showcase your success and accomplishments that make you relevant for your next role.
- For your previous roles, it's really important to include your achievements, e.g. awards or attendance to Presidents Club.
- Showcase your certifications. These not only demonstrate

your accreditations, but your dedication to learning and improving your skillset.

Style, format, tone

- Define your value proposition: Have an engaging headline – not just a job title but the value you provide. To make your 'About Me' section compelling, start with a client-focused question, and include a value statement with delivery metrics and something personal.

- Set your tone: While it's important to make your profile stand out, authenticity is paramount. Your LinkedIn presence should reflect what you want prospective employers to know about you; including posts and likes.

- Maintain a degree of professionalism on LinkedIn; share thoughtful and useful content, don't mistake it for Facebook. This goes for the image you present of yourself as well, including your profile picture, which should be a good quality, professional headshot.

- Content creation: Develop a Point of View within your field. Don't be afraid to post content – as your career develops, so will your PoV and expertise, and others will want to learn from you. Focus on creating a presence you're proud of – you don't need to post all the time about yourself and your successes if that's not what you're comfortable with, just make sure you are using LinkedIn to share content that you think will be interesting and informative for your peers to read.

- Build your network: LinkedIn is ideal for connecting with other thought leaders and establishing your network.

- Amplify your voice: Make sure to showcase any thought leadership you have done – whether it be podcasts, blogs, panels etc – in your LinkedIn 'Featured' section. Don't be afraid to stand out, as long as you're truly showcasing yourself and your strengths.

LinkedIn can be a great tool to find a potential role. During any application process, researching the company, team, and hiring manager, as well as reaching out with a personalized note is a good way to show enthusiasm for a role. Of course, your messaging can and will change depending whether you are in work or looking for work. While in roles, people will often focus on presenting the company brand to attract more customers and prospects.

LYNDSEY REES-POWLES, AVP DIGITAL SALES AT SPLUNK, ON HOW SHE USES LINKEDIN WHEN HIRING

When hiring, I prioritize candidates who actively engage with their LinkedIn profiles in a way that showcases their expertise and thought leadership. I assess how often they use the platform and the nature of their interactions – whether they share insightful content, write informative articles, or engage meaningfully with others through comments and discussions.

LUCY: *For me, LinkedIn is a great place to showcase your expertise and to highlight what you can bring to an organization. When I am hiring I use LinkedIn extensively, because it allows an insight into how someone would represent the company and themselves.*

Resume/CV

Your resume is an opportunity to really show prospective employers who you are, what you have achieved, and to stand out from the crowd. If you haven't updated your resume (or CV) in a while, or are going for a role outside of your industry, it can be daunting to figure out where to start. So what are some things to keep in mind when crafting your resume?

- Remember that your resume is a representation of yourself, so make sure to always proofread it.
- Maintain a logical and consistent structure in your resume: no longer than two pages, consistently formatted, in a way that is easier to read and digest. Include section headings to break up the text and call out your achievements, with everything in a professional and easy-to-read font with immaculate spelling.
- Include a customized personal statement for each role or application: Why you? Why this role? Why now?
- If you're applying as a first-time manager, make sure that you highlight your key attributes and experience that demonstrates that you can lead – maybe you led a working group, or have good experience leading projects. Have you acted as a mentor, or been involved in training? In Part One we talked about attributes that lead to successful leaders, consider those: Are you able to resolve conflict calmly and successfully? Can you inspire others to perform well? Are you data driven? Do you have experience working under pressure?
- Provide data on what you have achieved, and do not leave anything up for interpretation. If applying for an AE or sales manager position, put the revenue or percentage of your quota attained. This should include:
  - Quota attainment each year (and whether it was ramped)
  - £/$ revenue booked (and Average Order Value)
  - Presidents Club years
  - Year on Year growth
- Split the above between new logos, cross sell and upsell. This information is essential, because it communicates that you know what you're doing, and you have the numbers to prove it.
- When referring to numbers, don't be tempted to exaggerate! Always make sure you are truthful. Sales leaders know

how compensation plans work, so they will recognize what is realistic and what isn't. They will also be able to check all figures against the year-end numbers online if the company is public, so they will know if something is false.

- Go to peers that you respect or mentors who you want to be like and ask them to review your resume – they could show you something that you're missing or highlight how to better reflect your skillset and performance. if you are working with a headhunter or recruiter you can also ask for their feedback as they will have an idea on what the hiring company is looking for

SOPHIE SMITH
Major Account Executive

+447234567890 ☎
sophie.smith@1mail.net ✉
London, UK ⚲

SUMMARY

Results-driven sales professional with a track record of exceeding targets and fostering growth, consistently achieving over 120% quota attainment. Proven expertise in securing new business, enhancing customer satisfaction, and driving YoY revenue growth through strategic cross-sell and upsell initiatives.

EDUCATION

Barden University
Business Studies 2012-2015

SKILLS

- Pipeline Generation and management.
- Data-driven decision making
- Research, account planning, and prospecting into key accounts.
- Cross-functional collaboration with entire GTM team.
- MEDDICC Certified.

ACHIEVEMENTS

- Presidents Club (2018, 2019, 2021, 2022, 2024)
- 2024: Fastest promotion to Majors in all AEs.
- 2022: #1 Enterprise AE
- 2021: #2 Enterprise AE
- 2020: #1 Overall AE
- 2019: #1 AE in EMEA
- Rookie of the Year 2017
- Completed Frankfurt Marathon 2024
- Completed London Marathon 2023

PROFESSIONAL EXPERIENCE

Major Account Executive
Waystar Royco | 07/2023 - Present
125% avg. attainment | £1.2M quota | £100k AOV
- Secured new logos accounting for 60% of total revenue, with significant contributions from cross-sell (25%) and upsell (15%) initiatives.
- Reduced average sales cycle duration by 12% improving efficiency and increasing revenue velocity.
- Drove 35% Year-on-Year growth in revenue through strategic targeting of high-value prospects and expanding existing client portfolios.

Enterprise Account Executive
Acme Corporation | 01/2021 - 06/2023
110% avg. attainment | £1.1M quota | £75k AOV
- Balanced new client acquisitions (50%) with cross-sell (30%) and upsell (20%) opportunities, increasing account penetration.
- Developed customer success stories that highlighted 200% ROI for customers, aiding in future sales pitches and credibility building.
- Achieved 30% Year-on-Year revenue growth, leveraging data-driven insights to identify key upsell opportunities.
- Recognized in the top 10% of the sales team for exceeding targets and contributing to team-wide success.

Account Executive
Dunder-Mifflin | 09/2017 - 12/2020
120% avg. attainment | £800k quota | £45k AOV
- Led initiatives that resulted in 40% of revenue from cross-sell opportunities, complemented by 35% from upsell, enhancing client value and retention.
- Developed 75% of my own pipeline.
- Consistently grew revenue by 25% Year-on-Year, utilizing a consultative approach to uncover additional client needs and opportunities.

MARINA: *In my opinion your resume (CV in the UK) is the single most critical document you will ever create. It's your ticket to the interview room and serves as evidence of how you present yourself professionally. When I encounter a CV with mistakes, it often leads me to skip the interview altogether. To make the most of your interview time and avoid getting bogged down in data, I highly recommend ensuring your resume aligns with your LinkedIn profile, eliminating any discrepancies or gaps. If you're applying for a sales role, it's crucial to clearly state your quota and attainment, highlighting key wins and specifying any ramp-up years. This preparation allows the interview to focus on your character, approach, and mutual fit, rather than just your track record (which should be the things that gets you in the room in the first place).*

LUCY: *I see CVs as personal marketing tools that allow you to showcase your qualifications, experiences and skills to potential employers. Since this is typically the first point of contact between you and your employer, it's your chance to make a great first impression.*

It allows you to concisely outline your education and achievements, helping employers quickly assess the suitability for the role. A polished and professional CV demonstrates your attention to detail, as well as your commitment to the application process.

Finally, this is your chance to differentiate yourself from others who may be going for a similar role. After all we are in a competitive market and anything you can do to stand out will be of great value to you.

As an extension of your resume, when applying for jobs, do not overlook the impact of a personalized cover letter. Cover letters are incredibly powerful tools that provide candidates with the opportunity to showcase their alignment with the role and the company. Unlike a resume, which primarily lists qualifications and achievements, a cover letter allows you to share your story and convey your enthusiasm for the position. It gives you the chance to connect your skills and experiences to the specific needs of the organization, illustrating why you are not just a fit on paper, but a perfect match for their culture and values as well. A well-crafted cover letter can capture the attention of hiring managers, demonstrating your genuine interest and helping you stand out in a sea of applicants. This is your moment to express your passion and articulate how you can contribute to the team's success, making it a vital part of your candidacy.

PENNY: *A few years back I needed to update my CV and decided to add in two quotes from my previous managers into my personalised cover letter, both which illustrated key skills that were needed for the role I was applying for. I got really good feedback from the hiring manager who liked seeing the validation from my previous line managers, and differentiated me from the others.*

INTERVIEWING

Amazing; you have secured an interview for the role that you want. Now what? The interview process is a real opportunity to set yourself apart from other candidates, and so it's important to absolutely nail that first interview, as well as any subsequent ones. Here are some tips to do just that.

Before the Interview

As they say, "fail to prepare, prepare to fail." Thorough preparation is essential, for anything from interviews to presentations. Here are some things every person should do before an interview:

1. Know the job description (JD). It will give you much of the information you need. They have already told you what they're looking for, so ready yourself to make it clear that you're the right person for the role. This will make it easier to answer questions in the interview, because you will know what areas to highlight in advance. If you are going through a headhunter, make sure you get a full debrief from them on a call. They will have gone into detail with the hiring person to understand the profile of their ideal candidate. They can also clarify areas that are not clear in the JD.

2. Know the company inside and out. Learn about their values and vision – this will help determine whether you align with the mission of the company. This is where the company website will be hugely helpful – it has most, if not all, the information you need, from values and culture, to leadership team, to top customers and their success stories, their financial results (for public companies), and their products. There is no such thing as knowing too much. If you're already in the industry, you can even speak to some of their customers to gain an insight.

3. Do your research about the people who are going to interview you. With access to the internet, there is a lot of valuable information and data available that can aid thorough preparation, on LinkedIn and beyond. What thought leadership and content have the interviewing panel produced? From this you will be able to see where they stand on DEI, GTM strategy, management style. You can also use LinkedIn to see if you have common connections who you might be able to leverage as a potential connection in the interview process.

With access to the internet there really is no excuse to not come fully prepared for any interview.

4.   Treat it like a sales process. As you would define your ICP when prospecting for customers, have the same approach when prospecting for a new role: what is your ideal company fit and ideal job profile? In your sales process your outreach is tied to a compelling messaging to the prospect – the same is true when you are formulating your messaging for a prospective job and company. As mentioned, preparation ahead of time is imperative – reach out ahead of the interview and share an agenda, and prepare questions you want to ask them. This shows initiative and ensures you get to talk about your strengths and why you are well-suited to the position.

5.   Be willing to volunteer referees to speak to. You cannot underestimate the significance of good, solid references. They can also be showcased on your LinkedIn profile, so anyone considering you can immediately see the value you have brought in the past. Having people advocate for you publicly is a strong indicator of your credibility and a huge vote in your favor.

6.   Connect with individuals throughout the organization to conduct your own discovery about the team dynamics and culture. This proactive approach will help you qualify whether the position aligns with your goals and values. Utilize the insights you gain to enhance your first interview, enabling you to ask informed questions and demonstrate your genuine interest in the role and the company.

PENNY: *Preparation ahead of the interview is so important, because the way someone prepares for the interview tells you how they would prepare for meeting a prospect. I remember being impressed by a candidate who went through our sales channel,* *attended a webinar, and got a demo of our product ahead of the interview. They were going for a sales manager position, and were not only able to bring a good grasp of the product to the interview, but also a point of view on the selling experience from the customer perspective and areas where the team needed improvement and coaching.*

MARINA: *As leaders prioritize maintaining a public profile to attract talent, there's truly no excuse for candidates not to thoroughly research and understand their hiring managers. Having participated in several podcasts and panels, I've observed a significant difference in the preparation of candidates who take the time to listen to what I care about and value – often just an hour spent tuning into a podcast can make a world of difference. These candidates not only gain a clear understanding of my values and what I seek in a team member, but they also have a better sense of whether we'd enjoy working together. This preparation sets them apart and creates a meaningful foundation for the interview process.*

In the Interview

Once you're in the interview, prepared and with a clear head, it is an opportunity to cement your credibility. So, here are some best practices for when you're actually in the interview.

1. It's important to have a talk track that accompanies your resume. If you have an excellent resume that tells the hiring manager that you're exactly the person for the job, but you can't articulate any of your wins in conversation, you're going to lose credibility. One thing we recommend to demonstrate your wins is to utilize the STAR framework. STAR stands for Situation, Task, Action, Result. As an example:

Situation: *Successfully secured a major deal with a new enterprise customer.*

Task: *Assigned a portfolio of new accounts to develop within my territory.*

Action: *Collaborated closely with my channel partner to identify key decision-makers, establish strategic introductions, and navigate the sales process effectively.*

Result: *Secured the deal within 60 days, driving significant revenue growth and strengthening the partnership.*

This format gives you a structure to articulate your successes and tell compelling stories about them. Having reference points for your experience is important to ensure the interviewer remembers your competencies and triumphs – but don't ramble. You only have a short time, so don't waste it.

MARINA: *Those who truly impress me during interviews are those who masterfully weave compelling stories into their responses, effectively highlighting the hiring criteria. In sales,* *storytelling is paramount – it captivates the listener and illustrates how your experiences align with the role. When candidates share their narratives in a way that resonates, it not only showcases their skills but also demonstrates their ability to connect with others, which is key in the world of sales.*

2.   As with your resume, make sure you use data to back up what you have said about yourself. Sales is all about numbers and results, so you need to be able to prove that you can do what you say you can.

LUCY: *I had a great experience with a candidate who came through recently. They had all of their achievements, including the numbers, on a printed sheet. They were able to talk through these, telling stories along the way of where things went well and where they didn't, and how they overcame any challenges. In a slide deck, they had 'What Good Looks Like', with where they wanted to go and their five year career plan mapped out. They also had the 3 Whys: Why the Company, Why the Role and Why them.*

To me, that's really positive because it means they're not just thinking about now, but the future, which is what I want to see:

3.   Be prepared to answer some of the typical questions you encounter in interviews, such as:

SAMPLE QUESTIONS FOR AN INDIVIDUAL CONTRIBUTOR:

- **Walk me through a deal that you've won/lost** *(what were the key things that made you win? What could you have done better? What did you learn from the loss?)*
- **What tactics/strategies do you use to build pipeline?**
- **Talk me through your numbers and attainment.**
- **How do you run your business?**
- **What are the key criteria you will use to determine what a good opportunity looks like?**
- **What happens when you have had a bad year?**
- **Talk me through a time when you've built and leveraged a Champion and how you built the relationship with value?**
- **Walk me through a time when you made a mistake at work and what did you learn from it?**
- **What gets you up every morning?**
- **Why do you want to work for this company?**
- **Why should they hire you over anyone else?**
- **What makes you special?**
- **What is it about X company that makes you most excited?**
- **Where do you think your biggest development opportunity is?**
- **Walk me through how you currently run your week.**

4. Earlier, we talked about the attributes that make people suited for sales. Use those when talking about why you are suited for the role! Be proud about who you are, and talk about what you would bring to the job. This is something we have seen to be lacking in female candidates compared to their male counterparts. Lean into your key attributes, like good listening skills, empathy, or strong communication, for example. Give strong examples of how you have used these traits in the past to be successful, and you will show that you have what it takes to get things done.

5. Ask intelligent questions, and have them prepared ahead of time. The interview isn't just to see if you would be suited to the role; it's for you to see if the organization is a good fit for you. You can learn more about the company and the responsibilities you may have. It is likely to be a several stage interview process, so treat them all like discovery calls. It also demonstrates curiosity to the interviewer, and tells them that you are someone who likes to have all of the facts.

SAMPLE QUESTIONS TO ASK IN AN INTERVIEW

- **What are the biggest risks to the success of the business?**
- **What are the biggest strengths and weaknesses in your team?**
- **If there was one thing that separated A Players from the rest in your team, what is it?**
- **What have been the common traits amongst your most successful team members?**
- **What are your growth plans over the next 1, 3 and 5 years, and how do you see the role evolving?**

---

6. Ask for feedback. You can do this at the end of an interview as well as afterwards. Not only does this illustrate for you how you can improve and where you might do better in the future, it demonstrates your investment in your performance and your eagerness to do better.

7. Follow up via email after the interview, just as you would in a sales process in order to close the deal.

MARINA: *Don't miss the chance to close the deal at the end of your interview. I learned this lesson the hard way – don't make the same mistake I did. I vividly remember an interview with a VP of*

EMEA from the early days of my career where I felt I had nailed all my answers and we had a great, engaging conversation. As we wrapped up, he asked, "Do you have any other questions?"

I replied, "You know what, I think I've covered everything, and I'm really grateful."

He followed up, "So, nothing else?"

I responded, "No…" And in that moment, I sensed his hesitation. He then asked, "Do you want the bloody job?"

"Agh! Yes! Do I have the job?"

From that day forward, I vowed never to make that mistake again. While you don't necessarily need to ask, "Do I have the job?" you can instead say something like, "Is there anything from this interview that gives you reservations about moving me forward to the next round or offering me the position?" This approach not only helps you secure the job but also provides valuable feedback, demonstrating your commitment to personal development.

8. While it is important to fully understand the remuneration for the role, particularly as you get further along the process and need to understand the OTE and commission structure, timing is everything. Doing this after you have fully conveyed the value you can bring to the organization and role is important. It's worth speaking to the hiring/talent team about this beforehand so you get an idea of what to expect, but it doesn't need to be mentioned in the early interview stages. To go about this the right way, seek to understand early on in the process who will be able to share this information with you, so you can ensure expectations align. We can't control everything when it comes to interviews, but we can control ourselves; how we act and the impressions we make. Following the steps above will allow you to do everything in your power to secure a follow up interview, and hopefully, the perfect sales role for you!

TIPS FOR WHEN YOU'RE SEEKING A LEADERSHIP ROLE

As we've said before, knowing your data is essential when going for a position in sales. In leadership, it's how you prove your success. While being a leader is complex, there are some key metrics you should know when applying for a leadership position.

<u>Key Performance Indicators:</u>

1. Team quota and attainment Year on Year and last four quarters
2. Year on Year team ARR growth
3. Team tenure and internal development
4. Stand out wins
5. Pipeline (coverage, growth, new markets)

Below are some questions you could expect when going for a leadership position:

IF THIS IS YOUR FIRST LEADERSHIP ROLE:

- What skills do you have that will attribute to making you a good leader?

- What evidence do you have to show you have displayed good leadership qualities?

- Do you have a proven track record of attainment and forecast accuracy as an IC?

- Is there anything you do outside of work which will help shape you as a leader?

- What would your 30/60/90 day plan include as you move into your first leadership role?

IF YOU HAVE BEEN A LEADER PREVIOUSLY:

- How would you describe your leadership style?

- How do you coach your team?

- Describe a situation where you have had to resolve performance concerns.

- How do you successfully hire, develop and retain AE's?

- What do you find most challenging in the role, and what is your key area for growth and development?

IF YOU ARE GOING FOR A SECOND-LINE LEADER ROLE:

(A) How have you built and scaled a high-performing B2B sales team in a SaaS/software environment?

What this reveals:

- Your hiring philosophy (Do you prioritize experience, coachability, or grit?)
- Your approach to training and enablement (Do you use a structured methodology like MEDDIC or SPICED?)
- How you align sales with customer success and marketing
- Your track record in improving win rates and reducing ramp time.

(B) Walk me through a GTM strategy you've successfully implemented. What worked, what didn't, and what did you learn?

What this reveals:

- Your ability to strategically plan and execute
- How you adjust strategy based on market conditions, ICP insights, and data
- Your experience with different sales motions (enterprise vs. mid-market, inbound vs. outbound)
- Your ability to collaborate with marketing, product, and customer success

(C) What is your approach to forecasting and driving predictable revenue growth?

What this reveals:

- Whether you rely on gut feel or a structured forecasting methodology
- Your understanding of pipeline health and deal velocity
- How you mitigate churn risk and expand revenue through existing customers
- Your ability to align sales targets with realistic quota attainment

---

So, equipped with the skills to land the job, the question becomes: where do you start?

How to evaluate if a company is right for you

When joining a new company or new role as part of your tech sales career, it's important to find the right place for you; where you can create impact and be successful. No two companies will be the same, and certain solutions will be set up to succeed more than others – but it can be difficult to discern what the right companies will look like. From start-up to a unicorn, each type of organization will have different benefits and challenges along with differing levels of maturity. Here are some aspects of the most typical organizations you will encounter in tech to help you make your decision:

	Start-up (>$10m ARR)	Scale-up ($10m-100m ARR)
	Early stage companies focused on delivering an MVP (Minimal viable product) & achieving PMF (Product Market Fit).	Companies that have achieved Product Market Fit and are now focused on scaling operations, revenue and market share.
Characteristics	▯ Often pre-revenue or generating minimal revenue. ▯ Operate with small teams and limited resources. ▯ Highly focused on innovation and testing ideas rapidly. ▯ Dependency on external funding (angel investors, seed funding, or VC).	▯ ARR often exceeds £1m and is growing at a rate of 20-30% YoY. ▯ Greater focus on organizational structure and processes to support growth. ▯ Increasing team sizes, with specialization roles (enablement, revenue operations and customer success). ▯ Likely to seek further investment / funding rounds to support expansion through acquisition or entering into new markets.
Key Metrics	▯ Burn rate. ▯ Customer Acquisition Cost (CAC). ▯ Monthly active users (MAU). ▯ New ARR (annual recurring revenue).	▯ Customer lifetime value (CLV). ▯ Annual recurring revenue (ARR). ▯ Churn rate and scalability of infrastructure.
Pros	▯ The work you do makes a huge impact on a business of this size. ▯ You are likely to work more closely with the founder. ▯ As the company is smaller, you can have more flexibility in your role (e.g. the wider territory coverage or a hybrid role like SDR / AE / Team Lead).	▯ There is a more established customer base with proven customer success. ▯ Supporting functions like customer success, marketing and rev ops are already in place.
Cons	▯ It can be harder to sell when no one knows your product or company. ▯ More likely than not, the organization will be trying to get Product Market Fit. ▯ There is less of a support network in companies of this size, with enablement, rev ops and marketing teams being very small or nonexistent. ▯ The speed of change in younger organizations can pose a risk, but it can also be rewarding.	▯ There may be huge pressure to grow ARR in a shorter space of time. ▯ The organization is still evolving and developing processes. ▯ There can be challenges as the organization integrates other companies, as you deal with different people, processes or tech.

	Mature ($100m+)	Unicorns / Pre-IPO
	Well established organizations with proven business models, predictable revenue, and a significant market share.	High-growth companies valued over $1bn or preparing for an IPO.
Characteristics	▯ Stable revenue streams (over £150m+ ARR). ▯ Strong brand presence and market recognition. ▯ Focused on optimizing efficiency, diversifying offerings, and defending market position. ▯ Acquire other companies. Think companies like Salesforce, DataDog, Microsoft.	▯ Scaling but operate with a mature structure. Have a strong global presence & highly diversified product portfolio. ▯ Focused on IPO readiness. ▯ Think companies like Stripe, Revolut, Canva.
Key Metrics	▯ Profitability, stable growth and share price (if public). ▯ NPS (Net Promoter Scores). Diversification of revenue streams.	▯ Valuation. ▯ EBITDA margin.
Pros	▯ Well-established organizations will have clearly defined processes and playbooks, making them a good place to learn. ▯ There is a prestige that comes with working for big-name companies. ▯ If you are starting a family, there are often more benefits in a larger company. For example, if it is listed, you can accrue stock, which will be a huge financial boost.	▯ Typically enjoying a wave of success and a flow of 'feel good' news as you win bigger customers and see growth everywhere (product, team, revenue, etc.).
Cons	▯ The high standards at this level mean there can be a pressure to perform.	▯ Growth can be a priority in these kinds of organizations, which can mean they saturate the sales teams with people, which can make it harder to make an impact.

MARINA: *From a financial standpoint – choosing a company and its corresponding stage largely depends on where you are in your life, the responsibilities you carry, and your personal objectives. It often becomes a balancing act between reward and risk, making it challenging to select the right opportunity. Personally, I see stock-based compensation as a valuable upside, and I base my decisions on the potential to enhance my earnings through on-target compensation and accelerators. In my opinion, these accelerators should be the primary focus for top performers especially at an individual contributor level.*

Given my current situation – having lower overheads with no children and a manageable mortgage – I feel well-positioned to take on greater risks by pursuing opportunities with earlier-stage companies. However, I also recognize the importance of a strong foundation, which is why I found WIZ such an appealing company. Their exceptional technology, talented team, and reputable brand within the industry make them an excellent choice. Ultimately, success is measured by the problems your solution addresses and its ability to deliver real value for your customers.

I also strongly believe the "people" aspect of the business is equally critical. I want to work alongside individuals who inspire me, challenge me, and ensure that I am continuously learning – plus being in a fun and engaging work environment.

PENNY: *I've worked for companies of all sizes – from a Series A startup striving for its first £1M ARR to Meta, and everything in between. Each stage brought different challenges, lessons, and experiences that have been invaluable throughout my career. Over time, I've realized that my sweet spot is scale-ups – companies that have established product-market fit, are experiencing profitable growth, and are at a stage where they can invest in systems,* *people, and scalable processes, often with an exit on the horizon. But beyond growth potential, what matters most to me is the culture and the people. I want to work with great people who align with my values – where diversity, equity, and inclusion aren't just buzzwords, but core to how the business operates and that the CEO and Exec team get behind.*

LUCY: *For me, choosing the right tech company is not just about prestige or funding, it's about aligning my skills, ambitions, and values with the stage of growth where I can make the biggest impact and thrive. The technology solution is also important to me, I need to find it interesting and exciting and also ensure it solves 'real world problems'. That's why I chose Datadog, as its powerful observability and monitoring capabilities help organizations detect, diagnose and resolve real life technical issues, such as performance bottlenecks in checkout workflows or preventing an organization's security breaches by tracking suspicious activity. Culture is also important, and from what I have seen it can change as companies grow bigger due to shifts in structure, priorities, leadership, and employee dynamics.*

No matter which way you lean, talent is in high demand within tech; recruiting talent is a major challenge for 58% of technology decision-makers.[39] In addition, we think there are four main aspects that you should consider when making a decision about what a great company looks like:

1.   Cultural fit
2.   Financial stability and on a growth trajectory
3.   Opportunity to grow and develop
4.   Demonstrable Product Market Fit

People and Culture

It is important to be working with people you can learn from and who can help you thrive. We spend a lot of time at work, and you want to ensure you work in a good place, with good people.

If you are looking to truly excel, make sure the company you choose has the high performance culture that you're looking for. A-players like to be around A-players – if you don't have that culture in a company, it can lead to frustration when you are surrounded by people who don't share your drive to succeed.

There are a number of ways you can dig into the quality of the people and culture in a company. One is their eNPS (Employee Net Promoter Score), which is a standard way survey to measure how happy employees are in a company, however it's always worth checking when it was taken and if the score represents the whole company or just the sales team(s). We would also recommend looking at Glassdoor reviews (and the company's response to the reviews), and ask to meet a team colleague in the interview process.

To get a sense of what a place is like, you can also reach out to people in your network who work there or who know people who do. You can do this through LinkedIn as well if you don't know anyone personally.

Another good indicator of team culture is asking to look at the average tenure of the employees in sales roles and how many have been promoted. A high turnover rate of employees could indicate a negative work culture, and similarly, somewhere with low chances of career progression could delay your growth.

PENNY: *I think a good barometer for a good leader is to see how many people from their previous organizations have followed them, as well as understanding their approach to people, development and coaching, as that is important to me.*

When considering a company, we recommend looking not only at your prospective manager, but the whole leadership team – particularly as you take more senior roles, since you will be working with the much wider organization, and in some cases the Exec team. The leadership team of any company is the North Star of strategy, culture and success so it is important to know who they are, their experience and their strategic priorities. Loyalty among the team is a strong sign of a good workplace culture and a team that thrives – do the people in leadership have a following of people who have come from one company to another?

Don't underestimate the impact that cultural fit can have on your success. Consider the culture of the company and if it aligns with your value and who you are. You are more likely to be engaged, productive and therefore successful when working in a company that matches your own values and surrounded by people from whom you can learn. This comes back to the fact that you will have your own values and things that are important to you, so you will want to see if the company aligns. If you feel that there is a culture match, you can ask the hiring team in an interview how they incorporate the company values into their day-to-day. This will highlight how actually ingrained these values are to the people.

A final aspect to consider when evaluating the personnel of an organization is the diversity, or lack thereof, in the team. How important is diversity in the organization? What KPIs do they have in place to increase DEI? Is diversity present in the leadership team, or is everyone of a similar demographic and background? How much they value diversity will shed light on what matters to them and how you would be treated within the company.

PENNY: *For me a key part of good cultural fit is how high up* *on the agenda diversity is. As a way to test this in the interview process I ask why DEI is important to them, and what steps they are taking to improve in that area. You can usually tell from their response if it's serious or just a 'box-ticking' exercise.*

Financial Stability

When evaluating a company, their financial situation is a worthwhile aspect to consider, particularly in start ups, and the kind of role you would be going for. The kinds of questions you need to ask will vary depending on the maturity of the company. When evaluating a company, understanding its financial health is critical – especially in a startup environment, where funding and cash flow dictate long-term viability. The key questions to ask will depend on the company's maturity.

For early-stage startups (Seed or Series A), assess where they are in their funding journey:

- Have they recently secured funding? If so, how much, and what does this mean for their runway (i.e., how long they can operate before needing more capital)?
- Who are their investors? Strong backing from reputable VCs signals confidence in the company's growth potential.

For later-stage startups (Series B and beyond), focus on scalability and revenue efficiency:

- What is their customer retention rate? (High churn can indicate shaky product-market fit.)
- How many AEs hit quota last year? (If fewer than 50% are achieving targets, it could point to deeper issues with product fit or sales execution.)
- What is their burn rate vs. revenue growth? Are they spending efficiently to scale, or burning cash unsustainably?

While market dynamics can shift, these indicators help you gauge whether you're joining a startup poised for growth – or one at risk of financial strain.

When it comes to public companies, you can look at their websites for annual and 10K reports. Consider: has there been a turnover at the executive level recently? Is there a private equity firm involved? If so, for how long? Since private equity firms tend to run in five year cycles, depending on how long they have been involved with the organization, they could be looking to exit, which could lead to a change in executive and board teams, or an upcoming reorganization. For you, this could determine the stability of your potential role.

Considering an organization's financial stability is a necessary element to ensure the exciting opportunity of a new job turns into something long-lasting.

Development Opportunities

The organizations to work for are those that recognize your potential, seeing not only your current contributions but also your future growth and the extent to which they're willing to invest in your development. Here are key factors to consider that highlight how much a company values learning and development:

- What does their onboarding process entail? Is it a once-and-done approach, or does it evolve and adapt over time?
- Do they offer a comprehensive learning and development platform?
- Do they have a Learning & Development budget to use for additional courses i.e. language, leadership, Masters programs?
- What is the ongoing enablement strategy?
- How do they invest in management training?
- What approaches do the company have to career progression and planning?

To build a successful career, seek out an environment where you can thrive, enjoy your work, and continuously learn while earning!

MARINA: *I always had strong ambitions and a plan for where I want my career to go, and the opportunity for learning and development in new roles is a fundamental criteria for me. I'm really intentional about ensuring that my leadership team is aware of my aspirations and the direction I want to take and qualify this hard in any new opportunity that I pursue. I prefer to work backwards with them to create a clear plan, identifying any gaps in my capabilities that we can address through one-on-ones, skip-level conversations, or coaching. This proactive approach has helped me grow but also needs to align to the company's goals, paving the way for my success and the success of the team and ensuring the business and the people in it are growing.*

LUCY: *Personal development and growth in any role is super important to me, and working for an organization that supports this forms part of my criteria. Success in tech sales is not just about hitting targets – it's about continuous learning, adaptability and mastering the art of selling. Organizations that invest in personal development empower their teams to evolve with the industry, drive innovation, and build long term customer trust, as well as allowing the employee to feel valued.*

The Technology Itself

As the economic landscape shifts, it is important to position yourself in a company that exists in the market as a 'must-have', rather than a 'nice to have' – one that is recession proof. There are ways to determine if companies have successfully established Product Market Fit, which is particularly important for early stage companies.

1. Strong customer feedback and advocacy (NPS of 15+)
2. High Product Usage (what is the number of monthly active users?)
3. Customer retention (95%+)

Tying this in with financial stability, this will give you a better degree of security than you might have when dealing with 'nice to have' softwares. Equally, when you are stepping into a new role in tech, you should consider whether you find the solution itself compelling and exciting – you need to be passionate about the brand and platform to sell it with authority. This is important as a sales person and sales leader as it will determine how much tailwind you have behind you to be successful. To learn more about an organization's product or solution, you can consult the ways customers talk about it and the value that it gives them; there will likely be testimonials on the company's website.

PENNY: *Success as a sales leader is as much about the technology and how sticky it is for the customer, as it is about how you drive excellence in your sales team and GTM strategy. If you are churning lots of customers, or they are not getting value from the technology it will make your job as a revenue leader that much harder.*

Everyone is different, and everyone's attitude to sales is different. Hopefully in this chapter, we have given you some guidance that you can incorporate into your own approach, and unlock your true potential.

Chapter 4: Landing the role

Craft a strong CV that highlights your skills, experience, and achievements concisely. Prepare for interviews by leveraging storytelling to connect your past successes with the role, demonstrating your impact with data-driven examples. Show authenticity and confidence while addressing potential concerns proactively.

Establish a strong professional presence by aligning your LinkedIn profile and resume. Showcase achievements, awards, and thought leadership while maintaining authenticity. Engage with industry content and network strategically to enhance credibility and visibility.

Assess the company's culture, leadership, financial health, and market position. Ensure alignment with your values, career aspirations, and long-term growth potential by engaging with employees and asking insightful questions during the interview process.

Chapter Five

CAREER PROGRESSION AND REACHING YOUR FULL POTENTIAL

The surest way to success is to have a plan. When you have tackled obstacles with diligent preparation and secured the role you worked hard for, it's up to you to really take ownership of your career. Whichever path you take is unique to you, and what motivates you and plays to your strengths. In this chapter we have laid out what is known as a 'well trodden' sales progression path, but recognize that it is not linear, and is different for everyone. Success is what you make it, no matter what route your career takes.

It goes without saying, but success doesn't happen overnight. We don't wake up one day with the skills and opportunities to propel our career forward, we have to continually invest in them. Forming connections and establishing yourself among your peers is a crucial part of progressing in any role, but especially in sales, because so much of the role revolves around making connections with people and constantly learning from them. While it may seem daunting, putting yourself out there and networking is key to getting you in the rooms you want to be in.

Visualizing your goals with a written career plan provides clarity regarding future decisions and direction, which in turn will increase your chances of success. Writing these goals down can solidify your focus, and keep in your mind's eye what you want to accomplish. As you progress, reflect on the goals from past years – did you achieve them? Why, or why not? It has been proven that the simple act of writing out your goals means they have a 50% higher chance of happening.

BUILDING A CAREER PLAN

Writing a career plan is largely about investing time and thought into where you see yourself in the future – whether that be at the end of the year or in three years time. We have laid out four areas around which you can ask yourself some questions. Your answers will help you formulate a well-thought out plan for your career.

1. **Self-assessment**
    » Identify your values and beliefs. What are you driving for: Financial stability? Work/life balance? Purpose driven work?
    » What are your skills and strengths? (Technical/Leadership/Operational)
    » What are your interests? (what type of work energizes you?)

2. **Set career goals: short term (6 months- 1 year), and/or longer term (3-5 years) .**

    » Make sure they are SMART goals (we referred to SMART earlier: Specific (clearly defined), Measurable (quantifiable), Achievable (ensure goal is attainable), Relevant (align your goal with your objectives). Timebound (give it a target date)

3. **Research opportunities**

   » What trends are there in your field? Is it growing/shrinking? Is that field oversaturated with talent?
   » Can you find mentors to support you?
   » Which companies align to your goals and are thriving?

4. **Develop an action plan**

   » What skills do you need to develop? (identify courses or certifications)
   » Networking goals (which events should you attend and which thought leaders should you meet)
   » Create milestones

SAMPLE CAREER PLAN

Current Role / Position	Your current title and responsibilities
Career Vision	Where you see yourself in 5-10 years
Short-Term Goals	Specific objectives for the next 6 months - 2 years
Long-Term Goals	Broader aspirations for the next 3-10 years
Skill Gaps	Skills or experiences you need to acquire
Action Plan	Specific steps to achieve your goals (e.g., courses, projects, networking)
Networking Goals	Specific steps to achieve your goals (e.g., courses, projects, networking)
Progress Metrics	KPIs to track success (e.g., promotions, certifications, feedback scores)

When shaping your goals, talk to people who have achieved what you want – what did they do? What can you learn from them? Don't be afraid to advocate for yourself.

So, what does a sales career path look like? How do you make the move upwards?

PHASE ONE: SDR – AE

While it's not the case for everyone, many top salespeople start out as Sales Development Representatives (SDRs). An SDR is pivotal to an organization, so if you get it right, the sky's the limit.

The SDR role is a great development ground for sales; it teaches you the importance of pipeline generation, discipline in qualification and prioritization of time, and introduces you to the sales playbook. It allows you to hone your communication skills digitally and on the phone, and gives you exposure to the product. As an SDR you will work cross functionally with marketing and sales, contacting customers and prospects and setting up meetings on behalf of the AEs. Not only does this give you an introduction to your customers, but it gives you a chance to work alongside more tenured sales professionals who you can learn from.

To be consistently achieving as an SDR you need to be regularly hitting your targets and providing value to the AE you are partnering with, or the wider team in general if you are responsible for your own business. What you can't learn by doing, you can learn from the AEs you support, if this is the case. You will have a clear insight into what they do, including but not limited to:

1. Account mapping and prioritization
2. Contact research and org chart building
3. Creating a hypothesis for accounts and outbound pipeline generation plans

4. Writing well structured outreach (we recommend the SCIPAB method)
5. Calling structures to include elevator pitches

With a view of where you ended to get to, you will get practical guidance from someone who has the exact experience you need. You will be able to see what a top performer looks like.

Moving from being an SDR into a closing role can be a bit of a leap, so use your time as an SDR to develop your skills. These skills can include account planning and how to research prospective customers to understand how you can align your solution to their needs, as well as simplifying that message and articulating that to a prospect in a succinct manner. An ability to stand out from the noise is key.

The attributes that make a great SDR often translate to those of a great salesperson. These include being proactive, organized, a good communicator, driven, resilient, and being data-driven. While some of these are innate, you can work to build them so you can transfer them to future roles, and be ready to excel!

LUCY: *SDRs hold one of the most important roles within the sales ecosystem; they also hold one of the hardest. If an SDR puts in the time and effort early in their career, they will begin to nurture the skills needed to be a successful AE. When my teams work with the SDR function, I encourage them to put time in, because what you put in is what you'll get out. On a weekly basis, not only do they spend time planning the outreach strategy, they will also offer guidance and hands-on coaching to ensure the SDR is feeling fulfilled in their role. At the end of the day the SDR is there to learn, they want to become sellers, so getting insight from tenured, successful sales professionals is a massive win for them.*

KEY SKILLS OF AN SDR:

- Grit and Tenacity
- Organizational and Time Management Skills
- Good Communication Skills

MARINA: *When I joined AppDynamics, I had applied for a Commercial AE role, but in the end was offered a BDR role. At first I was really disappointed, because it meant taking a step back to learn the basics. But it was the best decision I ever made; I used it as an opportunity to consider what I wanted from the role, and how I could convince the people who were hiring me to back me and invest in me. I reached out to the person who offered me the job and asked for an agreement that if I successfully hit certain goals that were way above my target that firstly I would be promoted, and secondly, I would be put in a team where I could learn from the best, because that's all I cared about at the time.*

So, as a BDR, I figured out that to hit 200% of my target, I needed four New Business Meetings a week. I approached my leader and asked if I booked those NBMs on Monday and Tuesday, if I could spend the rest of the week flying to different countries to shadow the reps, because I was working alongside some absolutely amazing sales professionals, and there was so much I could learn from them. To do that, I had to be super organized. The only way I ensured my success was making sure I worked harder than everybody else. I spent the week shadowing the best reps in the company and sitting in Quarterly Business Meetings (QBRs). I was just a sponge, asking questions and building my confidence. It can be scary to be a BDR in a company like that, but I built my confidence up and learned how to ask for help, which is what put me in such a good place now. Those reps that I worked for have remained close friends and advocates of mine through my entire career.

PHASE TWO: AE – FIRST LINE LEADER

In Part One, we discussed how going from an AE or IC position to leadership isn't for everyone. It's a shift from being 'me first' to 'team first'; you're taking on everyone's number, not just your own. It's about coaching, mentoring, and developing the people in your team.

If you are at this stage of the book, and this is the step you want to take, you need to remember when moving into a first-line leadership role, that what motivates you as an individual contributor to be successful isn't going to be the same for everyone. Find your own authentic leadership style and take into account the different personalities within your team. As a leader you will ultimately want to gain their trust and see them thrive. In order to do this you will need to find ways to engage with each of them. The best teams are those full of different people with different perspectives, but that means you'll need to inspire them in different ways. That also goes for how you communicate with them – some of your team may prefer hopping on a quick call to discuss something, while others would rather you just sent them a message. Tailoring your approach to the individual will allow you to get the best out of each person.

Having a high-performing team all starts with a vision, and getting your team to trust that you can help them achieve that vision. Of course, trust needs to be earned, and that will come with time as you consistently show up for your team and help them to do what no one else has done. When it comes to leading A-players, they need to be challenged so they can learn. If you don't challenge them, or create an environment of trust, they won't learn, and they will leave!

To truly lay the groundwork for success, you should seek training and other opportunities to improve your leadership skills. Good companies will invest in their front-line leaders, and if they do not there are many courses out there, and you can likely ask the company for that investment – it will pay them back in dividends! When individuals and companies invest in management training and coaching for new managers, new leaders can hit the ground running.

Many people who make the step from IC to leadership end up managing people who were their peers. Here are some tips on how you can ensure that team will respect you as a leader:

- Be transparent. Make it clear that all you want is to help them be better at what they're already great at, and how you plan to do just that.
- Remember that you wouldn't be in a leadership role if no one believed in your ability to lead.
- Maintain open communication. Talk about why you're moving into the role and what you bring to the team. You can also rely on the team, using them as a sounding board, because being the leader doesn't mean you necessarily know more than anyone else.

LUCY: *I think there are lots of things to consider when you go from peer to leader of the team. When I moved into my first leadership role, where I was managing people I'd been in a team with, I took each of them aside in a one-to-one to ensure they were supportive and to understand what they wanted from a leader. It can be challenging, especially when someone else in the team went for the same role. Ultimately, you need to start as you mean to go on and make sure that the team is in the boat with you.*

MARINA: *The best advice I ever got was: when you seek out the first leadership position, make sure it's one that has an element* *of velocity. This means being involved in a variety of deals that have momentum – while they may not be the largest deals, they offer valuable learning experiences. Engaging with multiple opportunities allows your brain to develop muscle memory for navigating challenges, responding to questions, and coaching others effectively.*

A NOTE FROM FLAVIA BROWN, AVP AT MULTIVERSE:

I always aspired to make the move into leadership. When I stepped up, I was the most senior salesperson on my team and I was already supporting others, so while it did happen earlier than I expected it made sense. However, the transition was much harder than I anticipated, especially in those first six months. One big change was losing control of my diary – as an AE, you are autonomous and you manage your time, but as a first line leader, you're in back-to-back customer and AE meetings.

My biggest lesson? Avoid the urge to "super rep." It might feel helpful to close deals for your team, but it creates dependency, limits their growth, and can lead to your burnout. True leadership is about empowering people to succeed – even if it means letting them fail occasionally.

Recruitment is also new and exciting. It's the most important decision you make, worth 150% of your AE's quotas. One mishire can have a gigantic impact on your team and results. It's not just about identifying great talent but also building your personal brand so you attract them. Ensure you are clear on why someone should work for you as a leader, as well as your business. You will need to take risks, but understand what are the acceptable levels of risk and build a plan to support that individual in those areas during their ramp.

Leadership has its challenges, from being the main culture carrier, managing stress, and fielding team emotions and concerns. But in my career, there is nothing more rewarding than being a first line leader and seeing someone grow from X to Y under your development. That beats closing any deal.

PHASE THREE: FIRST LINE LEADER – RVP/VP

When you step up from first-line leadership to a second line role, the learning curve is slightly less steep than that first move into leadership, but the focus shifts. As a second line leader (like RVP or VP), you are typically responsible for three first-line leaders or more, who will each have teams below them. The way these teams are differentiated can vary; it may be divided across geographies, functions (like SDR teams or Sales Operations) or sales motions (like Midmarket or Enterprise).

To step into second-line leadership, you need to have proven successful at business management. Have you demonstrated an ability to lead your team to get consistent results? Are you able to predictably forecast and help your team do the same? Has your team been able to deliver from pipeline to progression to closing? Through consistently hitting your number quarter on quarter, and by understanding the measurements that drive that success, you will demonstrate that you can clinch the revenue aspect of sales leadership.

However, another key difference in these roles is that you are not just about one particular sales team anymore. You can't put on your 'super rep' hat as you might have as a first-line leader, or else you risk your leaders losing credibility. You move from being team-focused to business-focused, which continues the more senior you get.

A mistake typically made in the transition from first-line to second-line leadership is the failure to understand or engage with cross functional teams or the broader business. At this new level, you are responsible for a much wider ecosystem. A lot of your time is split between people management, forecasting and cross functional alignment. It's important to take a step back and understand how everyone in the wider ecosystem is motivated, so you can understand how you can work together for the good of the overall business.

A difference when moving to second-line leadership is that you will need to work upwards more; you will be reporting into those above you, perhaps the C-suite, to be certain of your numbers and data. Senior stakeholder management gets added to the mix of your previous responsibilities. You also might need to be in more meetings and do more reporting. To do these successfully, organization and prioritization are essential.

The details you are involved with will change as you move away from managing and coaching a set of ICs to ensuring that team leaders are on the path to hitting their KPIs and that the cross functional revenue leaders/teams are aligned to the deliverables as well as communicating to the SLT/execs on what support is needed, what the successes are and what the plan is.

Having a strong set of leaders beneath you is crucial. That means not only hiring great people, but coaching people to best coach others. With that comes trusting your leaders to know what they are doing, develop them, and to solve problems that benefit that wider ecosystem. That includes shielding the team from noise that might not be relevant to what they're doing, ensuring that external or non-sales functions are working well with the team, and that overall, everyone is rowing the boat in the same direction.

Another mistake people make when they first move to second line leadership is forgetting that their job is to develop leaders.

Investing in your leaders with training, playbooks and best in class processes is critical to their success and that of the sales teams. It can seriously level up the sales teams' performances, so working with your enablement team and managers to coach is an important step.

As a second-line leader, it's important to shift your thinking from "My job is to make sure my reps can do this." to "My job is to make sure my leaders know how to do and train this." When this is established, it helps with retention as you are helping your team become the best leaders they can be. That includes shielding the team from noise that might not be relevant to what they're doing, ensuring that external or non-sales functions are working well with the team, and that overall, everyone is rowing the boat in the same direction.

A WORD FROM JASON CREANE, VP AND GENERAL MANAGER AT VARONIS:

The advice I tend to offer first-line leaders who are stepping up into second line is... take the time to develop your sales leaders and learn how your cross-functional teams can support you and your team. To gain control over a larger business, the tendency is to revert to working alongside the first-line leaders and manage deals with the ICs. This consumes a huge amount of time and can limit your ability to focus on developing your leaders and gaining more value and scale from your cross-functional teams and partners.

MARINA: *One of the mistakes I made when I went into second line leadership was not involving people in key decisions – even if the decision doesn't necessarily sit with them, making them feel part of the team can make a world of difference when it comes* *to incentivizing them to work with you. Instead of just creating a plan and positioning it to them, get people on board by building the plan with them. Remember that they're not just working with one leader at this level, and what you're fighting for is your unfair share of those people's time and their willingness to work with you over other people, so it's important to make that good for them.*

PENNY: *One of the things I have learned about moving into second or third line leadership is how important it is to build a strong team of talent around you, quickly. Having a strong unit as a leadership team is so important – knowing our collective and individual team goals, and being able to rely on each of the leaders to be accountable and deliver on their commitments ensures success as a group.*

To excel as a second-line leader, there are always new things to learn and improve upon. This could include building relationships with those outside of the sales sphere, or making sure that all marketing activities are followed up on, or finding out the best practice to use data to accurately see how much marketing activities influence deals, for example.

What makes a great second-line leader, and thus a great team, is the ability to develop and clearly articulate a vision that gets the entire team pulling in the same direction. What makes the real difference are those who don't simply set a direction one day and gather the team to get them motivated and think that will drive change. It's those who spend considerable time invested in figuring out what the root causes of the inefficiency or ineffectiveness in their current operating rhythm. With conviction of what needs to change in order for things to improve, they figure out how to convince others with data and stories about those issues. Being transparent with your team is what will open their eyes to it, and then you can paint a picture of what change can look like on a micro level, and thus what the future could look like on a macro level. By taking them on the journey of how that change will be achieved, you inspire them to adopt that vision for improvement.

LYNDSAY REES-POWLES, AVP DIGITAL SALES AT SPLUNK, ON MOVING INTO SECOND-LINE LEADERSHIP:

Transitioning into second-line leadership, I faced the challenge of stepping back and trusting my team. As someone who tends to be hands-on, it was essential to allow those in leadership roles the autonomy to lead and learn from their experiences. For instance, when one of my managers considered hiring a candidate I felt wasn't suitable, I reminded him, "It's your team to manage. I'll share my perspective, but the decision – and any consequences – are yours." He ultimately chose not to hire that individual. This experience underscored the importance of clearly defining our respective roles and allowing each other the space to perform them effectively.

Effective delegation is crucial in leadership. It involves entrusting team members to make decisions, fostering their growth and confidence. However, it's important to avoid micromanaging, which can hinder team development and morale. Striking the right balance between oversight and autonomy is key to building a successful team. In second-line leadership, it's essential to manage upwards by proactively engaging with senior management especially in Sales supporting functions such as Digital Sales or Marketing. This involves assertively seeking involvement in key discussions and ensuring open communication across departments to break down silos. By doing so, you foster collaboration and contribute to the organization's overall success. Effective cross-functional collaboration is crucial for achieving shared goals and driving innovation. Leaders should encourage open communication, establish clear objectives, and build trust among teams to enhance collaboration. This approach not only improves team performance but also aligns efforts towards common organizational objectives.

PHASE FOUR: GETTING TO THE C-SUITE

Getting to the C-suite – whether that be as a CEO, CRO, CCO or COO – takes drive, resilience and determination. It takes not only being good, but being excellent at what you do. For women at C-suite level, there can be a feeling that you need to be better than your male counterparts to have the same opportunity. All the while, you may still face the same microaggressions and challenges faced by women throughout their career, despite being senior in the company.

A key factor in getting to the C-suite for your first CRO role and succeeding while you are there is having an internal sponsor – someone at the executive level who champions you. In addition, having an external coach or mentor, preferably a seasoned CRO or commercial leader, can provide critical guidance. They help you identify where you need to improve, and can be the voice reassuring you when you doubt yourself.

While as a second line leader or VP is primarily focused on hitting sales targets within a specific region or segment, a CRO oversees revenue across the entire business. This means the role extends far beyond sales – reporting on critical metrics like LTV/CAC, NRR, New ARR, and overall company growth.

As an Exec, the CRO is also heavily involved in broader business strategy, which would include acquisitions, funding rounds, and potential exits. This means regular interaction with investors, board members, and other executives. To succeed, you need to think beyond "running sales" and focus on the full revenue ecosystem, ensuring scalability, operational efficiency, and long-term profitability.

When evaluating CROs, companies typically look for three things:

- A proven track record: success in a similar-sized firm, with consistent delivery on revenue targets and Year on Year growth.
- Leadership capability: proven track record in attracting, retaining, and scaling high-performing teams across multiple functions.
- Strategic alignment: an ability to clearly articulate your management style, an understanding of cross-functional teams (Marketing, Customer Success, Rev Ops), and cultural fit within the executive team.
- Being data driven: leveraging data and AI to bring increased efficiency in the sales process, decrease cost of sale, and track trends in your customer buying process to know where to optimize.

Many consider the CRO position to be one of the most demanding roles on the executive team. With an average tenure of 18 months for CROs, it is clear to see that often the buck stops with them in terms of sale – a mistakenly common view being that only sales are responsible for growing business rather than the entire revenue function (Product, Marketing, Customer Success, Support and service).

As an Executive it requires a combination of resilience, strategic thinking, and relentless prioritization. You will be involved in a large number of the company's strategic objectives, so it is important to focus on impact, clarity in direction and to be aligned with the rest of the executive team.

As you become more senior it is more about getting the systems and processes in place that can scale growth, and leveraging data across the entire revenue chain to know where to optimize across a larger more complex GTM organization.

Building your network will be critical as you work towards a revenue leadership role. When you move to any company, you will want to surround yourself with good people quickly. So, being able to tap into a trusted network will speed up chances of success. Some of the highest performing CROs come with a black book of strong leaders across sales and ops they can rely on, along with defined playbooks and processes they can quickly implement to get quick success.

PENNY: *One of the biggest shifts I experienced when moving from a VP Sales role to the C-suite was the change in dynamic – going from reporting into a manager to operating as a true peer within the executive team. As a CRO or CCO, no one is going to tell you what to do – you have to be bold, trust your judgment, and work with the other Exec team members to drive the whole business forward. The CEO is still the ultimate boss, but the team is accountable to the Board and Investors to deliver on your agreed commitments.*

Unlike a VP of Sales, a CRO isn't just responsible for closing deals – they're responsible for all revenue, which means marketing, product, and customer success all need to be aligned and performing.

The other big adjustment? Communication. At this level, it's not just about driving numbers – it's about managing expectations, refining your message, and sometimes delivering tough news in a way that doesn't spook investors. You spend more time with Finance, ensuring the plan and reporting are rock solid. And, of course, there are a lot more meetings – weekly Exec sessions, quarterly Board meetings, multi-day strategy planning offsites, as well as your own team meetings and 1-1s. Strong time management, clear communication, leveraging data to see trends, and a steady hand under pressure aren't just nice to have – they're essential if you want to succeed as a CRO.

FIONA MCCLUNE, CRO AT STRUCTUREFLOW, ON BEING A CRO:

I have been asked many times (mostly by family) what on earth the difference is between a VP Sales (previous role) and a CRO. My thoughts on this: A VP of Sales is the Ted Lasso of revenue – motivating the team, executing the playbook, and making sure everyone believes they can win.

My perspective: A CRO, however, is part strategist, part firefighter, part therapist, and part fortune teller – constructing the revenue engine while it's already hurtling down the track! And if you're a female CRO? You're leading revenue strategy – while people keep mistaking you for the event planner.

But – female leaders have the advantage. It's precisely our intuition – that deep-seated, nuanced insight – that sets us apart. My advice? Embrace and hone this intuition. Surround yourself with those who challenge you. Celebrate your wins (because they might go unnoticed otherwise). Trust your instincts, and never let a bad month make you doubt a solid strategy. Your intuition is your North Star; let it guide you. You are more powerful than you know.

As the numbers have shown, there are fewer women than men

in the C-suite. We've already talked about the significance of rectifying this, but it bears repeating: having more women in senior positions like CRO is critical for women across the organization. Not only do they act as someone that other women in the organization can aspire to be like, but they bring a different perspective and approach to leadership. On top of that, having more women in senior leadership attracts more women to the profession. Having more women in the C-suite signals to women throughout the company and beyond that they too can ascend the ranks and triumph.

NOT ALL PATHS ARE LINEAR

The career path that we have outlined throughout sales roles is simply an example; it is not the only way that you can progress through revenue roles. You can take a number of different routes to get to the role you want – and what you want might change throughout your career. Certainly, some people move from SDR to AE, onto first line leadership and so on, but others may take different paths, going from AE to Enablement, or into Customer Success.

Revenue is no longer just sales. It takes a village, namely Marketing, Presales, Sales, Enablement, Revenue Operations, Channel and CS, to grow a company's revenue. In fact, experiencing different kinds of roles in a variety of industries will make you more well-rounded, something that would hugely benefit you in a leadership role. Interacting cross-functionally is made a lot easier when you know what their day-to-day responsibilities look like. There is no 'one way' to pursue a sales career, or to enter leadership, and no route is better than any others. If you hone your skills and work hard, keeping your goals in mind, it will be a rewarding journey – and don't forget to enjoy it!

WHAT MAKES A GREAT LEADER?

Great sales leadership isn't about having all the answers – it's about empowering your team to find them. The best leaders create environments where people thrive, not just hit quota. At the heart of this are three essential skills: coaching mastery, clear and consistent communication, and a data-driven mindset. A great sales leader knows how to coach their team to develop skills, build confidence, and continuously improve. They communicate a compelling vision with clarity, ensuring cross-functional alignment and inspiring their teams to follow. And they don't just rely on gut feel – they track key metrics, spot trends, and use insights to make smart, informed decisions. These three pillars separate average managers from transformational leaders. Of course, they're not the only things that make a strong leader – in Part 1 we discussed some of the key attributes that make great leaders. But mastering these three fundamentals will not only drive results but also create high-performing, engaged sales teams. Whether you're an aspiring sales leader or looking to elevate your leadership game, focusing on these areas will set you apart.

<u>Communication</u>

To truly be the best sales leader that you can be, the way you present and talk about yourself and your business is crucial. While you might not know it, the way you communicate can accelerate or impede your team's success. The language we use can have a serious impact on how you are perceived by those around you.

For example, studies have found that women are much more likely to use self-deprecating or 'softer' language in the workplace; doing things like ending sentences with "if that makes sense?" or qualifying your requests with "just".[40] When we use this kind of phrasing, we can undermine what we are saying and imply that we aren't certain about it. This hesitation to commit in the language we use is a form of passive communication.

Of course, everyone has their own communication style – it is just important to keep in mind that the way you communicate should be authentic to you and the environment you are in. We have found that men, particularly those in sales, tend to be more assertive communicators. This often leads to them commanding more authority in a room, and subsequently they are listened to more than the more passive communicators around them.

When we communicate with assertion, we communicate with confidence. If you think you could benefit from being more assertive in your communication, here are some quick tips:

- Use 'I' statements – this conveys your thoughts or wishes without sounding accusatory. For example, you can say, "I'm confident that…" instead of "You're wrong."
- Be prepared when you can be – not just about what you are going to say but making sure the point you want to raise in high value conversations is well thought out.
- Control your voice – speak clearly and slowly, avoid rushing your words. This will convey that you are in control. Vary your tone as you speak; variation conveys interest and enthusiasm.
- Be consistent in your communication. Ensure your messaging is clear, reliable, and aligned with your values and actions.

A necessary element of communication, when you're a leader, is ensuring you give feedback in the most productive way. There is nothing worse than generic feedback that is not actionable. Give feedback in the moment, both positive and negative. When we try to mask constructive feedback with positive feedback, the listener senses the inauthenticity.

AS SAID BY STEPHANIE MACLAURIN, HEAD OF SALES AT BIRDIE:

When delivering feedback, it's about understanding how best to give that message; it's your responsibility to see how that feedback lands. If you give positive feedback but then follow it with constructive feedback, they will think the positive is fake.

ADAM QUARTERMAINE, SVP OF EMEA AT HARNESS THINKS:

If you want people to take feedback well, isolate instances where you give them praise. They can then get that constructive feedback later.

HAZEL KOCH, MAJORS AE AT ZSCALER, SAYS:

When you have a great leader who gives it to you straight, consistently, then you know they're always going to be genuine, that they'll give you the good and the bad. It's really refreshing. Being authentic is what makes it land.

Another fundamental aspect of communication is active listening. It builds trust, strengthens relationships, and ensures that both team members and stakeholders feel heard and valued. True active listening isn't just about hearing words – it's about being fully present, resisting the urge to formulate a response too soon, and demonstrating genuine understanding.

A simple technique is to reflect back what you've heard: "It sounds like you feel/want/think… Did I get that right?" This confirms understanding and helps retain key information. It also gives the person you're talking to the chance to say yes or no, and helps you ensure you get a true understanding of what they want. Misinterpretations often arise from assuming we understand before someone has finished speaking. By listening with an open mind, leaders can uncover deeper insights and foster more meaningful conversations.

LUCY: *I think that so often leaders can talk too much, and it's just for the sake of being heard. What I do now when I'm on a team call or a customer call, I give myself five 'coins' to use for interjections or questions. Once they are gone, unless it's super important, I try to give the team the chance to run the call or meeting as they want to. I do the same for internal meetings; giving myself five opportunities to ask questions makes you use them sparingly. Obviously there are exceptions, but they're just that: exceptions, not the rule.*

MARINA: *I have a Post-It note on my wall that reads, "Active Listening." It serves as a constant reminder that active listening opens the door to summarizing what we've heard and playing it back in a concise and insightful manner. Not only does this deepen understanding but also builds credibility, showing customers that you truly value their input and perspective and their importance. Listening is an undervalued skill in a world of zoom and a hundred distractions.*

Mastering active listening allows leaders to set the tone for open and productive communication. It allows us to get our point across and ensure that what we are saying matters to the person we're speaking to. Furthermore, it's a skill that strengthens team dynamics, and ultimately drives better outcomes for the whole organization.

Data Driven

Being data-driven as a software sales leader means minimizing risk by making informed decisions based on metrics and insights rather than intuition. A sales leader is ultimately judged on hitting their forecasts and targets. Embracing a data-driven mindset involves tracking key performance indicators like sales velocity, conversion rates, and customer engagement to optimize strategies and forecast accurately.

By focusing on leading indicators instead of just outcomes, sales teams can create a more predictable and scalable revenue engine. A data-driven approach improves pipeline visibility, enhances accountability, and ensures teams prioritize the highest-impact activities. Ultimately, it enables consistent growth, sharper decision-making, and a more efficient sales process in competitive markets: all essential components of being a successful leader.

PENNY: *I am a firm believer in the saying "You can't manage what you can't measure." I am not saying listening to your gut isn't important – it is – but as a sales leader you 100% need access to data to not only survive, but to thrive in this job. When you are a VP Sales or CRO you can find yourself in one of two positions: either drowning in ldata, or not having access to enough. Either way, knowing how to identify what needs 'fixing' in your sales pipeline (is there a sales enablement problem, or a lack of quality leads, or misaligned targeting) is really hard. So having the right CRM set up, and the right KPIs to consistently track, alongside a badass Revenue Operations person is key to your success!*

Coaching

Great sales coaching goes beyond developing an AE's skills – it cultivates the right mindset and execution strategies to drive sustained success. Exceptional coaching isn't about providing answers but asking the right questions to encourage critical thinking.

It involves regular 1-1s focused on deal strategy, pipeline health, and skill development rather than just monitoring activity. Strong coaches use structured frameworks to help reps diagnose deals, identify risks, and improve qualification. They provide real-time feedback, reinforce best practices through role-playing, and refine messaging for better customer engagement. Coaching should be personalized to each AE's strengths and areas for growth to ensure continuous improvement.

The best leaders foster a culture where feedback is embraced, learning is ongoing, and reps take ownership of their development. Effective coaching isn't about micromanaging – it's about empowering AEs to become strategic, self-sufficient sellers. When done well, it leads to higher win rates, shorter sales cycles, and stronger overall performance.

No matter how gifted a seller or leader you may be, as you progress in your role you will need to develop and learn new skills. Working on your skills and leveraging them to the best of your ability will allow you to hone your craft as a sales professional, and give you what you need to reach your full potential – and more!

Chapter 5: Career Progression and Reaching Your Full Potential

The best way to ensure progression and growth is to have a career plan. Within that, you will have milestones and actions to ensure you stay focused on continued learning, networking, and timelines.

Transitioning to leadership requires shifting from individual achievements to team development. It's about finding ways to motivate different people not only within your team(s) but also cross functionally.

Career progression in sales doesn't have to follow a traditional linear path. Individuals may transition between roles like AE to Enablement, or from leadership to individual contributor roles, depending on their goals and the skills they wish to develop. Exploring diverse roles and industries can make professionals more well-rounded and effective, particularly in leadership positions.

Chapter Six

CHALLENGES OF BEING A WOMAN IN SALES

Though the landscape is constantly changing, as it stands, sales is still a largely male-dominated industry, particularly as you advance through the ranks. A study from Gartner found that despite making up 50% of entry level sales roles, only 30% of senior sales leaders are women.[41] Many women in sales and sales leadership roles have had experiences where they have been the only woman in the room.

In an environment like this, there are bound to be challenges encountered by women which, if unaddressed, are intensified for those looking to go into sales leadership. Many of us are incredibly capable of surmounting these challenges, but we should all work to make the sales environment more welcoming to women who want to pursue a career in sales or sales leadership. The aim of this chapter is to identify some of the obstacles that disproportionately impact women – not to complain or to place blame, but so we can collectively work to solve them.

UNCONSCIOUS BIAS AND MICROAGGRESSIONS

While the effects of explicit bias and the way it manifests may seem more obvious, it has been found that more ambiguous bias and subtle, everyday discrimination can be more detrimental to people's performances.[42] It is hard to quantify, but the constant second-guessing and questioning oneself can be quite taxing, which as a result can have a negative impact on people's performance.[43]

Unconscious bias hinders women in the workplace, especially when it manifests as microaggressions. This is a problem exacerbated for women of color; compared to their peers, including other women, Black women leaders are more likely to have their competence questioned and to experience disrespectful or degrading treatment from colleagues.[44]

Many female sales professionals feel they are not taken seriously due to their age or marital status. Married sales women were wary of telling employers they were married to avoid a perception that they would then want to leave the job to start a family. Conversely, unmarried sales women confessed to feeling like they were viewed as much more junior.

PENNY: *By the time I was in my late twenties, I had consistently been a top performer in my company for a number of years. I had a call from a headhunter who was representing our main competitor wanting to hire me. A day before the meeting I was told the meeting was cancelled. It turns out they found out I was 'at that age' where I might have children so they decided to pass. The irony of this was that it was a number of years later before I had children, and when I did I remained top performer in both of those years. How short sighted of them!*

Unconscious biases around the role of women in the workplace and what is considered a "woman's job" also means that in many workplaces, not just in sales, women are asked to do more miscellaneous administrative work than their male colleagues. We did a survey in a room of female salespeople, and found that nearly half of them had been asked to take the notes in a meeting, and several shared stories of being the person expected to tidy the office or organize the snacks. What's almost worse is that when asked, many women will do this work because they do not want to be labeled 'difficult to work with'[45] or 'not a team player'.

This is a criticism leveled almost solely at women; a study of 248 performance reviews found that women receive negative feedback that men simply don't. We can likely attribute this to further unconscious and unchecked biases on how women are "supposed" to behave. These biases mean that women are told to "watch their tone", to "step back"; they are called abrasive, aggressive, and emotional.[46] Successful female leaders are often ones who exhibit what may be considered masculine traits. However, those traits, which are praised in male leaders, become grounds for criticism in their female counterparts. A female CEO is not confident, she is narcissistic. She is not assertive, she is bossy. When the word 'aggressive' appears in male performance reviews, it is with the encouragement to be more so.[47] Women are not afforded the same luxury, instead they are called bitches, ballbreakers. Encountering biases that paint them in this light, women are not made to feel welcome in positions of leadership. This can make it difficult for women looking to enter sales leadership.

A 2023 Women in the Workplace study of corporate America by McKinsey found that women experience microaggressions at a much higher rate than men. For example, they are often not taken seriously and are almost twice as likely as their male peers to be mistaken for someone more junior.[48] Overall, women are more likely than men to:[49]

- Have their judgment questioned
- Be interrupted or spoken over
- Have someone else get credit for their ideas – 37% of female leaders have had a coworker get credit for their idea (versus 27% of male leaders).
- Feel pressure to change their appearance to look more professional
- Tone down what they say to avoid being unlikable[50]
- Had detrimental comments made about them behind their back (what they look like, their emotional state)

Microaggressions can have a significant impact on women's overall experience in the workplace; women who experience them are 4.2 times more likely to feel burned out.[51]

Other obstacles that come with being a woman in a male-dominated space are exacerbated due to an inability to discuss them. Typical 'women's issues' like hormonal changes, menopause and struggles with childcare leave many women at a loss because in a predominantly male space they often feel they cannot talk about them. Though they are simple facts of life and nothing to be ashamed of, many women do not feel comfortable talking about them, even when they may impact their work life.

MARINA: *In my experience, interruptions can be really damaging to culture and confidence, especially in settings where women are underrepresented. During my time leading a team in the Middle East, I frequently encountered meetings where interruptions were the norm, to the point where it became demoralizing. When someone speaks over you or dismisses your input, it not only invalidates your perspective but also undermines confidence and dampens enthusiasm.*

I've seen situations where someone is sharing their thoughts and someone loudly dismisses their idea without truly listening, it not only invalidates your perspective but also dampens enthusiasm and confidence. Often, the quietest voices hold the most valuable insights.

PENNY: *Something I've encountered a number of times is saying something in a meeting to my colleagues, only to have a male counterpart explain the exact same thing in a different way and be greeted with lots of nods and agreement, almost as if I hadn't said anything. It got the point where I started to question my communication style, assuming it was all on me. It was only when I spoke to the women that almost all of them felt the same*

LUCY: *I have had numerous occasions over the past 25 years where a good idea, template or document has been taken by someone else in the team or company and paraded as their work. Sometimes they have even forgotten to take my name out of it and replace it with their own. This can be very frustrating, awkward and slightly embarrassing... for them...*

ANNIE ANONYMOUS: *When I am in a meeting with an audience of predominantly older men, I often switch a ring I'm wearing to my ring finger, or put one on intentionally. I've found* *that by doing this I am taken a lot more seriously, and don't feel as self conscious.*

PENNY: *Years ago, when I was in an entry level sales role, we had an offsite in Colorado in the middle of their hot summer. The evening activity was a barn dance, BBQ and drinks. I wore jeans and a vest top (not revealing but sleeveless). I will never forget being pulled aside by a more tenured sales leader suggesting that I should dress more appropriately and that they had spoken to my manager to offer me some financial support to buy more appropriate clothes. I was mortified.*

ANNIE ANONYMOUS: *I have been pulled up on my tone before. A woman's tone can be taken very differently from a man's . I was in a QBR and my boss pulled me up about something I said, saying that I sounded really bitchy, however when a guy made the exact same comment ten minutes later nothing was said. Men are often celebrated, whilst women are berated.*

LUCY: *I was asked to be on a company website to advertise diversity within the career section, and I was asked to provide an image and a quote about working for the company. In the picture I submitted, I had a bright colored V-neck top on, but when I looked at the image when it was made live, they had edited it to a beige, high-neck top. For me I felt disappointed they made this change, without even making me aware.*

BRO CULTURE: DOES IT EXIST?

On the surface, bro culture is a subculture that arises in male-dominated spaces that prioritizes men of a certain type whose behavior alienates their female colleagues. The behavior that arises in these environments tends to be quite exclusionary towards female colleagues. Often, this isn't intentional. By nature, we are drawn to those like us. As humans, that is how we traditionally form communities. It stands to reason that in companies with a largely male workforce, that a kind of 'pack mentality' occurs.

ANNIE ANONYMOUS: *Recently, during an EMEA leadership meeting I didn't attend, a group of 10 men spent 20 minutes discussing me negatively, both professionally and personally. A female colleague who overheard the conversation informed me of what was said and who was involved. This made me feel so self conscious each time I saw or spoke to any of them as I knew they were very nasty about me behind my back. My confidence has been knocked and I am really struggling to get over it. It also creates an environment that I am not supportive of as an employee, as I doubt I'm the only target of such discussions. One day, when I am confident enough I will address it with the parties, as I would love to see the look on their face when they know they have been found out!*

ANNIE ANONYMOUS: *I remember being part of conversations with male colleagues in after work drinks where they would quite openly rate female coworkers out of 10 on how they looked or who they would sleep with. Looking back I should have said it made me uncomfortable, but I was concerned at the time that I would be judged as 'too serious' and it would have pushed me even further out of the group.*

However, when we create an 'in-group' made-up of people with similar belief systems, looks, or opinions, there will always be an 'out-group' as a byproduct of that, and this doesn't have to be about gender.

Behavioral science has proven that the anterior cingulate cortex, the part of your brain affected when you are excluded, is the same part of your brain that is affected by physical pain.[52] What this means is that when you exclude someone, it is the neurological equivalent of punching them in the face. So, while to many, a boys' club cama-raderie, complete with in-jokes and gate-kept knowledge, seems harmless, it can have a real negative effect on the women in the organization, and perhaps others who are not part of this 'in-group' – they may not want to contribute in meetings, or present in front of an entire room of men. Studies have shown that these kinds of environments are less attractive to both men and women[53], but still a 2021 report from TrustRadius found that 83% of women in tech sales worked at a company where bro culture was pervasive.[54]

Sometimes the way bro culture manifests is as simple as not including the women in social outings, but it can also arise in a multitude of ways. It can look like WhatsApp groups, full of male employees only, where they talk about specific women in the business (and never in a flattering or respectful manner). It can equally include the way the men speak to their female colleagues, often using language that they would never use with their male peers. Or it might be something as seemingly insignificant as con-stantly interrupting their female colleagues; a 2015 study found that on average men interrupted women more than twice as often as women interrupted men.[55] In the world of sales as it is, too many women in sales encounter this toxic atmosphere.

A WORD FROM HAZEL KOCH, MAJORS AE AT ZSCALER:

So often, as the only woman in the room, I'd end up being part of conversations that were incredibly disheartening; discussing professional women's bodies, other women in the industry, discrediting their achievements, and attributing promotions to diversity hires – I've experienced all of these things many times over. And because I was outnumbered, I remember quite a few times where people would say, 'Well, you're just one of the guys, right? This all stays between us.' It's the idea that, in order for me to be accepted in a professional setting where I'm the only woman, I need to be more like those around me. I need to leave what sets me apart at the door.

PENNY: *My first President's Club was in the US, and I was really excited as I was the top performer in EMEA that year. Being the only woman there out of 150 attendees didn't bother me but it did mean that the events and banter were pretty male-centric. The primary activity for the two days was golf. Sadly, I was one of the minority that didn't play golf, which ultimately meant I missed out on valuable networking time with the Exec team. The nature of having over 80% of the org spending their days playing golf created an 'in group', with golfing jokes and recounting stories of the day. At the time I remember almost being annoyed at myself for not having learned to play golf, but as I have grown I look back at this and realize that this was unacceptable, and that it was in fact the duty of the company, and leaders, to create an inclusive environment for all – where there are activities that bring teams together, not small groups or individuals.*

ANNIE ANONYMOUS: *I have worked for a lot of companies and there is always a boys' WhatsApp group, where they organize breakfast, drinks down in the pub, or just to bitch and talk about others behind their backs.*

There was one instance in the industry where people lost their jobs due to a specific WhatsApp group's content being found out, where they were discussing a woman on stage at an event in a derogatory way. There should be zero tolerance to these groups, especially when the leaders are involved.

When things like this happen, many women will not know where to turn to discuss these attitudes or behaviors. Or, if they raise it with their male colleague, they just don't spot the behavior or the damage it can cause. Often they will not want to say anything that could be construed as complaining, because they don't want their careers to be affected. It can particularly be a problem when the behavior isn't direct. When bro culture manifests in the subtle undertones of constant comments, in not being included, in being made to feel inferior, or like a *woman*, not an equal, like in the examples above, it can feel impossible to tackle.

Of course, the impact of this goes past day-to-day work life. Since the mindset that thrives in this atmosphere is not one that looks kindly on women, women's career progression is set back (as touched on previously); female leaders are more likely to report that they were denied or overlooked for a raise, promotion or other career opportunities due to being a woman or being a mother[56]. Overall, bro culture, which unfortunately pervades the world of sales, can deter women from pursuing a career in which they would otherwise thrive.

LUCY: *Sometimes, bro culture can actually have an opposite effect and be positive, as those excluded will just get on with their work. When I joined one organization, the boys' club had breakfast every day until 10 am, which I was not invited to. Meanwhile, I was in the office for 8 am, so by the time they joined, I was two hours ahead in work. I managed to get so much more done in that time, was effective and productive and quarter upon quarter I outperformed them all. Sometimes you just need to make good out of the bad.*

It is worth pointing out that things with bro culture have improved in recent years. Many leaders, both male and female, make conscious efforts to discourage bro culture-like behaviors. Additionally, several people we have spoken to who experienced things on the more extreme end of the bro culture spectrum agree that those kinds of things would never be tolerated or even happen nowadays.

In Part Three, we will cover the ways organizations can make women feel more welcome and included in order to retain more women, but here are some things that organizations and managers can do to combat bro culture:

1. Unconscious bias training should be mandatory across all organizations annually.
2. Call out bad behavior when it is seen, and make examples of it.
3. Managers should build teams that are truly diverse, with an understanding of why diversity is key, and make sure to foster inclusive hiring practices.
4. Establish and enforce clear values, including a code of conduct.
5. Lead by example.

MARINA: *I absolutely refuse to tolerate bro culture, whether it's groups ganging up on someone or engaging in backchannel conversations on WhatsApp. I find this behavior not only dangerous but detrimental to the team, and I make it a point to call it out whenever I see it. As a leader, I often address the situation directly, "I'm not sure what you hope to achieve by discussing this behind someone's back, but I want you to know that I'm aware of it. If you have something constructive to say, bring it to me directly. If not, then let's keep it to ourselves unless it serves a purpose." Simply confronting this behavior can catch people off guard and make them reconsider their actions, as they realize it won't be tolerated.*

It's crucial to create a culture like this and also to have crucial conversations to shut this kind of behavior down fast, that way everyone feels safe and respected.

COMPETENCE VS. CONFIDENCE

In sales and other industries, we have observed that there tends to be a competence/confidence gap. Women who are highly competent may lack the confidence to match, while some men who are highly confident lack the matching competence.

For example, in our experience, someone who makes big statements in an internal meeting with no data to support it (which you know aren't correct, because you actually know the data). When you're unaware of what you don't know, it can seem like you know everything.

In 1999, psychologists David Dunning and Justin Kruger of Cornell University discovered the eponymous Dunning-Kruger effect. In their study, they argued that individuals with significant gaps in knowledge or expertise may struggle to recognize their own limitations. Or, essentially, the effect implies that those who lack competence are often unaware of their own shortcomings.[57] Since then, many psychologists have tried to understand the cause of it, but we think that many of us have encountered it in our day to day.

While we hesitate to make generalizations, this is something that is likely more prevalent with men, as recent research has shown that while women typically evaluate their intelligence realistically, men with average intelligence often believe they are smarter than the majority of people.[58] Ergo, men are more likely to have a confidence in their abilities that is not matched by their competence.

When you work with someone like this, it can impact your entire team because often the loudest voice in the room is considered the most competent, and so other people, who might be just as competent, will go overlooked.

On top of that, when someone is nearing incompetence but remains so unabashedly confident, it makes it very difficult for someone else to be the one to challenge them for fear of sounding argumentative. If it is a woman challenging a man and it gets heated, in some cases she is then condemned as emotional, rather than just attempting to make a point.

However, while over confidence or lack of awareness of one's ignorance may cause issues, many people can be held back by their confidence not matching their competence.

LUCY: *Something that has still given me a fear of presenting to this day is something that happened when I was twenty-two. At a kick-off everyone had learned the corporate pitch, but I was sick in the hospital after an allergic reaction. The next week, they picked someone out of a hat to present it in front of everybody, and it was me. Although I probably knew it, the fact that I hadn't been in the sessions to learn it and it was in front of an audience of 100 people meant my confidence was absolutely knocked and I absolutely buckled.*

After the pitch, the leader at the time questioned whether I was capable of doing my job as the corporate pitch was really important for gaining new customers. It was seen as very black and white: can she do it, can she not?

This year, I had to get on stage at a kick-off in front of about 2,500 people, and I actually had hypnotism to try and help me with that fear, because my confidence is still affected by it. Thankfully, it worked because I got up there and I did it. I know that I'm competent, but 100% I can be hampered by my confidence.

Many women in sales and in sales leadership underestimate their talents, even when they are the one people around them look at with admiration. An obstacle many of us encounter is the disbelief that we deserve to be there in the first place, due to societal pressure or gender norms. A 2020 study from KPMG found that 74% of women in executive positions believe that their male counterparts do not experience self-doubt as much as female leaders do[59]. For many women, we can see the gap between who we are and who we want to be, and we assume everyone else can see that as well. This lack of confidence can cause women to hold themselves back, while their male counterparts have a running start.

PENNY: *It's funny how someone can perceive themselves so differently to those around them. I have always had a tendency to focus on things I need to work on rather than my successes. I am working on trying to recognize when I do things well, but am always surprised and flattered when someone sings my praises.*

Confidence in sales is instrumental to continued success. We all know that when you win one deal, you are more likely to win the next one; success breeds success. That's why we see people 'on a roll' in sales – their success pushes them to more success.

LUCY: *Confidence in sales leads to success repeatedly because it directly impacts how sales people communicate, build relationships, and handle objections. Customers are more likely to trust and buy from someone who speaks with confidence and conviction and knows their business inside out, it also reassures buyers that they are making the right decision. Confidence can also help sales people control their conversations, ask the right questions and guide their customers towards a decision. In the world of sales, objections are inevitable; a confident sales person does not get discouraged by these, but as Marina mentioned earlier, addresses concerns head on and turns them into opportunities. There are multiple ways* *you can build confidence in sales such as mastering the product, understanding the technology inside out, practicing through role plays and real life experiences and adopting a growth mindset, learning from failure to refine your approach. Confidence will be key to your future success.*

WE ASKED OLLIE SHARPE, CRO AT TRUMPET, ABOUT THE IMPACT OF A LACK OF CONFIDENCE:

I think that, sometimes, if somebody lacks confidence, it will impact their success, in a number of ways. I did door-to-door sales when I first started, and if you'd already sold at the last three doors, when you go to the next one you'll show confidence, and chances are you're going to sell that one. Confidence actually drives success, and you want them to have confidence in what they're selling and their own ability – if someone turns up with a product and is like, "Yeah, it's okay," you're not going to buy it.

IMPOSTER SYNDROME

When we lack confidence in our competence, we open the door for imposter syndrome. It can stem from the feeling that everyone around you knows more, which means you might not feel comfortable to step forward with your opinions, which only holds you back. Imposter syndrome, as its name suggests, is the feeling that you are a fraud or an imposter. You doubt your abilities and skills, and as a result, you don't feel like you belong in the position you hold. It can both come from a lack of confidence and damage your overall confidence.

For women, imposter syndrome is not rare, in fact, it is incredibly common; a KPMG study found that 75% of female executives across various industries have experienced imposter syndrome in their careers[60]. Of course, it's not something felt solely by women; it affects people regardless of gender – it can just manifest differently.

Different things can trigger feelings of imposter syndrome. For many women, the discrepancy between what they expected from their career and its reality made them feel like imposters[61]. Why would such a gap exist when many sales leaders are ambitious and career-driven from the get-go? We can likely attribute part of it to one of three things:

1. There is some preconditioning in women, particularly when they are young, that can make them more risk averse to avoid failure.
2. Without female role models in sales, women coming up will be less likely to believe they belong there.
3. While paving your way and being among 'the first' can be invigorating, it can also be intimidating.

ANNIE ANONYMOUS: *I have imposter syndrome daily. It's something that eats away at me, and I am forever second-guessing myself, my capabilities, and whether what I am doing is right. The big change from being an individual contributor to being a leader is that your decisions are no longer just impacting you, they impact the team around you, above you and below you; you can't really second guess yourself, and you have to believe that you are in a role because you can do it. Easier said than done a lot of the time, but it means you go above and beyond to ensure that all bases are covered and that you have the right information. I think imposter syndrome makes you prepare to the nth degree. That's always a positive, imposter or not.*

PENNY: *I am not a big fan of the term 'imposter syndrome' but I have definitely experienced feelings of doubt that have made* *me question myself. I try to not let that inner voice get too loud as it can be destructive, and as I have progressed in my career I have realized the feelings associated with 'imposter syndrome' are not always a bad thing. If I am pushing myself out of my comfort zone and surrounding myself with great people, then there is an expectation that I will feel uncomfortable but I know that is a good thing – it means I am learning and growing. In recent years, I have dialed down the negative internal dialogue, and have more faith in my experience and myself.*

However, a slight sense of imposter syndrome is not always a bad thing. Let's look back to Dunning-Kruger. Rather than being ignorant and going about the world assuming we know everything, many of us would say we want to know where we can improve. When you recognize where you have gaps in your skillset or knowledge, you can work to fill them in and consistently improve your performance.

MARINA: *I view imposter syndrome as a significant advantage in leadership and high performance. Although it can be uncomfortable, it drives me to leave no stone unturned. It compels me to thoroughly prepare and educate myself, ensuring I'm the most knowledgeable and well-prepared person in the room. This diligence often leads to better outcomes, as I'm equipped to tackle challenges and respond to questions with confidence.*

I think it also gives people a sense of humility and self-awareness that is invaluable for effective leadership. It encourages me to remain open to feedback, recognize my limitations, and seek input from others, which ultimately strengthens me as a person and leader. When leaders openly acknowledge their uncertainties, they create an environment where team members feel safe to express their own doubts and seek help, promoting a culture of learning and growth.

I also think not knowing everything can spark innovation and creativity. When I feel uncertain, I'm more likely to explore new ideas and perspectives.

LUCY: *I read somewhere that imposter syndrome is actually healthy; you should have imposter syndrome every three to six months because that's what drives your growth mindset. So I do wonder, is it a bad thing or does it push you to continue to self-develop? I think that's probably what it does for me – if I think that I can't do something, I'll then go buy a book on it to read about it, talk about it with others who may be able to help, and then execute to try and overcome it.*

The more I think about it, imposter syndrome has given me the motivation to improve, to learn new skills, and to focus on attention to detail, not only because I don't want to be wrong but because it gives me a deeper understanding of my field and ensures I have a commitment to excellence. I want to counteract any feelings of inadequacy, so I go above and beyond to make sure everything I do is as good as it could possibly be.

A WORD FROM JASON CREANE, VP AND GENERAL MANAGER AT VARONIS:

Imposter syndrome isn't reserved for women. I think it's something that we all experience and it's a natural thing to feel when you are uncomfortable. In fact, arguably it should be viewed as a transitory feeling; something that you experience for a set period of time until you start to build up confidence in your job. But having imposter syndrome to begin with probably gives you an indication that you're doing the right thing because you're doing something that you don't feel prepared to do, and doing things you're not prepared to do is a great way of growing.

While it might not come easily to many of us, confidence is pivotal to success. This is not to say that women should fake confidence, nor that they should have a false sense of their abilities, but rather that they need the confidence to match their competence. Not only that, they deserve it. This is especially true in leadership roles – while you may be recognized by your superiors as having the skills to lead a team, when you have that faith and confidence that you can succeed, you do the best for your colleagues and for yourself.

But how do you foster that confidence? How do you overcome that imposter syndrome? Sometimes, validation from others and seeing the successful results can help. Being recognized for your work goes a long way to boosting confidence; for example, having a supportive performance manager was named a key factor in reducing feelings of imposter syndrome.[62] When you're in a leadership position, seeing your team hitting targets and thriving in terms of culture and in promotions can prove to you that you are providing value. So potentially, you can overcome it just by putting your head down and doing your job, and the confidence will follow. But what can you do internally?

SOLVING IMPOSTER SYNDROME AND BUILDING CONFIDENCE

Normalize It

When you recognize that imposter syndrome is incredibly common across all levels of sales and sales leadership, it becomes easier to tackle. If we talk openly about imposter syndrome, struggling with it and overcoming it, it will become a lot less taboo. Many women in sales will be less likely to think, "Oh, someone else could probably do this," and instead think, "Okay, everyone feels like this sometimes, I'm not alone." Once you acknowledge that feeling outside your comfort zone is something many people face, you will be able to recognize it when it rears its head, and you can stop it in its tracks.

After all, a degree of imposter syndrome or lack of confidence is only natural when we step out of our comfort zone, which is a necessary step in order to progress. If we feel uncomfortable doing something, it usually means we're doing or trying something new, and that is important for career progression. It can also mean that you care a lot about doing something well, which is never a bad thing. If we never step out of our comfort zone, if we never feel that imposter syndrome, we risk stagnancy, which does no one any good. If we normalize that feeling of imposter syndrome, we encourage people to put themselves in situations where they might feel uncomfortable. Once they've done that, who knows what they can achieve?

Positive Inner Voice

The way you speak to yourself matters. Over the years, a variety of sports psychologists have studied the effects of 'self-talk' on athletes' performances. The resounding results, as you might guess, prove that talking negatively to yourself will diminish your performance.[63] In addition, they found that positive self-talk will have the opposite effect, even when compared with just neutral thinking. So, not only should you avoid speaking negatively to yourself, the data says you should actively be speaking positively if you want to improve your performance.

Utilizing a positive inner voice can also help you to counter those imposter syndrome feelings as it helps you to master your emotions. Pretending something doesn't exist is no way to make it go away. Instead, you should acknowledge how you feel, so you can course-correct. If you find yourself thinking, "I feel out of my depth" or "I don't belong here" don't just push that thought away. Accept your feelings, and engage that positive inner voice to change them. Remind yourself that you deserve to be where you are. Think: I feel like that because I'm being challenged, but I can handle this. You are skilled and the company hired you because they believe in you. Remind yourself of times you have felt this way before and successfully come through. Every time these thoughts creep into your mind, you need to be disciplined, as almost a daily practice and it will gradually improve. When you look back at what you've accomplished in the past, it will become clear that you are fit to be where you are. You may have forgotten how awesome you can be because as women we are often encouraged to be modest. But you don't need to be held back by that. Own your successes! Make sure you spell out what you have achieved in your mind as part of that positive self-talk.

Be Vulnerable

As women in sales, particularly in leadership, we can sometimes feel like we need to have all the answers, and that we need to solve our problems ourselves. But that's not necessarily true. It is okay to be vulnerable, to turn to leadership and peers, and speak about how you are feeling. With them, you can uncover why you feel that way, and how you can counteract it. You can draw on data to analyze your performance, and they can give you real advice, feedback, and opinions on what you can do to overcome your sense of imposter syndrome and highlight what you do well that you might not be aware of. You can also return the favor, and share what your colleagues and peers do well to equally build their confidence. Ultimately, being vulnerable as a leader with your team is essential to building trust, as it helps your team feel safe, and able to fail. For example, sometimes that vulnerability can look like admitting to not having the answer sometimes, and letting your team help you.

MARINA: *Vulnerability is a powerful asset in sales and leadership; it helps fosters genuine connections and builds trust with clients and team members. When you embrace vulnerability, you show authenticity, which encourages openness in conversations and strengthens relationships. I am obsessed with all things Simon Sinek and he always says, "There is no courage without vulnerability." Through acknowledging our challenges and uncertainties, we create an environment where others feel safe to share their own hurdles and in sales, often those are the gaps and risks that need to be addressed. I think as a sales leader or salesperson, embracing vulnerability allows us to build stronger rapport, collaborate better, and ultimately drive greater success for ourselves and our teams.*

LUCY: *I have someone in my team who struggled being vulnerable in front of male leaders, but was okay doing so with me. They saw it being vulnerable in front of men as a sign of weakness.*

FROM FIONA MCCLUNE, CRO AT STRUCTUREFLOW:

> *The moment you go to someone you respect and ask for help and say, "I'm doubting my ability to X, Y and Z," it's just natural for them to not only give you encouragement, but to remind you: You're fine, you've got this. Remember why you can do this, because of Z, and I saw you do this and that. If you are vulnerable with them, they will help you get rid of that imposter syndrome.*

Stand Tall

Throughout the 2010s, power posing rose to prominence. The idea behind it is that when you present yourself openly and expansively, you will feel more powerful, and ergo more confident. Power posing has been a subject of debate in psychology, but the central tenet remains true: your physical presence can be incredibly impactful on your confidence. When you shrink yourself in front of others, you are affecting how you are perceived, both by them and by yourself. So, when interacting with colleagues and clients in person, stand tall and hold your head high. For important meetings, stand at the front, don't hide behind your colleagues. When public speaking, look at the audience. Speak articulately and slowly, more so than may feel comfortable as the likelihood is that if you are nervous you are speaking more quickly than you think.

PENNY: *I get really nervous before public speaking, so I have developed a few tricks that help just before I go on stage to give me that extra confidence boost. I always make sure I am dressed in a way that makes me feel good, I make sure my voice is warmed up so it doesn't croak and I can project, I make sure I stand tall, shoulders back as I walk on stage, and I listen to some uplifting music just before to give me a spring in my step and SMILE.*

In video calls, where building rapport and conveying personality are more challenging, your presentation setup is critical. It's crucial to ensure you are presenting from the screen with the camera, avoiding distractions like looking away or multitasking. Maintaining focused eye contact and minimizing background noise by silencing all notifications helps you come across in a better way and actually is probably quite different to how other people show up.

Have Courage in Your Convictions

When you first start out in leadership, it can be daunting when you go into a room and you're the newest person there. It can be even more daunting when you're the only woman. It can often feel like you need to be just like your male colleagues to do the job correctly. But all this does is feed into that imposter syndrome and that lack of confidence, because you aren't like any of your colleagues, you're you! Trying to emulate anyone else will only be inauthentic and hinder your confidence. Instead, focus on developing your own leadership style.

You should be confident in how you present yourself to others while maintaining your authenticity. Don't be afraid to embrace the 'difference' that comes with being female, but don't let it hold you back either. Be sure and clear when communicating your point of view, using data points where needed, and the impact will be immediately palpable. While at first, when everyone is discussing a problem, and you spot a solution that feels obvious, you might not speak up, because you think, "Okay, maybe I don't have as much experience as everyone else, so I won't say what I really think," you are doing yourself and those around you a disservice. Having courage in your convictions is incredibly important, because actually, your fresh approach, ideas, and perspective are invaluable to the rest of the management team. Once again: remember that you're there for a reason, and your opinions do matter.

ANNIE ANONYMOUS: *When I first joined a company, we had a weekly Global Sales call where the first 15 minutes was talking about the sports scores from the weekend. It then proceeded to be 3 or 4 very loud men talking about themselves and their wins and how they do things for the next hour. There were no diverse voices on the call, unless it was marketing talking about an event. As a woman, this made me really switch off to the content, which is a shame as I know some of it would be useful. I found myself turning the volume down.*

I brought this up with the leadership and it was acknowledged and it was changed for a short while, but they overcorrected and I am sure that had the opposite effect.

Life is about balance, it need not be all one way or another. For me the key is showing diverse opinions and why it is important. If you are a revenue leader who runs GSCs, really think about how you can make them useful for the entire audience, and show you have a diverse and successful sales team across the board.

LUCY: *Putting myself out there with our previous CRO and talking about the importance of women in sales and leadership led to me being asked to co-lead the Women of Datadog community guild. We have the largest, globally diverse group and it is truly rewarding to see elements of togetherness and how much everyone is creating a much broader network and helping each other; I never would have created an internal sponsor had I not spoken up.*

A lack of confidence will hold anyone back in sales, but especially those who are already at a disadvantage. What we must remember is that being different can be a superpower. As women, we bring fresh perspectives, diverse outlooks and new approaches to the table. Having high EQ and empathy can help us to build strong relationships and trust with customers, quickly. Our different points of view allow us to have different conversations, often yielding better results. For women in sales, as an example, our resilience that comes with working in a male-dominated field translates to persistence in getting to our goals and the ability to adapt to challenging circumstances. As a result, we can inspire others to persevere when they might be dealing with obstacles.

At the end of the day, your career is in your hands, for good and for bad. How you go about pursuing success is up to you, so it is your responsibility to do the best you can. Work hard – while the environment can be tough, you're tougher. Build your skills, keep your goals in mind, and embrace that you are different from those around you – everyone is!

Chapter 6: Challenges of Being a Woman in Sales

Women in sales often face biases, such as being mistaken for junior roles, interrupted, or undervalued. Certain workplace dynamics, like informal exclusions, marginalize women and limit their career growth. Leaders can actively foster inclusivity by amplifying the contributions of women in meets and ensuring fair and unbiased promotion practices that recognize talent and potentially equally.

Overconfidence without competence can harm teams, while women often undervalue their abilities despite strong skills. Striving for confidence that matches competence fosters effective leadership and career progression.

Imposter syndrome, common among women leaders, can be mitigated by practicing positive self-talk, seeking feedback, and embracing vulnerability. These strategies help build authentic confidence and counteract self-doubt.

Chapter Seven

CRUCIAL CONVERSATIONS

The book *Crucial Conversations* defines such a discussion as one involving two or more individuals who have conflicting viewpoints on a critical issue, with strong emotions influencing the conversation.[64] While these absolutely are relevant in your personal life, they can have a serious impact on your career. Whether it's a promotion, a pay rise, or taking parental leave, success lies in the navigation of the conversation. Since there's a lot at stake, it's important to make these conversations go as well as possible – which can be hard to do if we're unprepared and don't have a model of what good looks like. That's why in this chapter, we're going to look at how best to maneuver the conversations that are critical to your sales career.

PLANNING A FAMILY AND TAKING PARENTAL LEAVE

When we asked people how they felt about talking to their manager about being pregnant and needing to go on parental leave, pretty much everyone said the same thing: they were incredibly nervous; about the impact it could have on their career, or about the potential negative impact on their income.

PENNY: *I was really nervous when I told my manager that I was pregnant with my first child. At that time, I was a successful enterprise AE and the key accounts I'd built over the last five years were generating really good growth. My concerns at the time were twofold: first, what would happen to my commission on the deals I was working on since half my earnings were commission-based, and second, would I lose my accounts while I was on leave? I will admit he did not handle it well initially and immediately panicked as to what potential revenue would be at risk! However I worked out a handover plan and agreed cover on my accounts with him while to mitigate any revenue that worked well"*

Depending on the size of the organization, what that conversation looks like will vary. Most companies will have parental leave policies, so it's always a good idea to understand that when you are hired, along with the other benefits. This conversation *should* be straightforward, but always go in prepared. Know your company policy, if you don't, you can speak confidentially to your HR partner.

If you are in the situation where there is no maternity policy in place then research your country's statutory maternity rights, and ask peers in other companies that are a similar size what policy they have in place. For example, in the UK, all employees are entitled up to 52 weeks of maternity leave, and if they return after 26 weeks or less, they have the right to return to the same job with the same terms and conditions.[65] Knowing this as your baseline and building from there based on your research in other companies is a good place to start. Helping them to get a strong policy in place will not only support you, but be an important part of a wider way to attract and retain more female talent.

It's worth having a conversation with your leadership team about maternity policies long before you're planning on having children.

Stephanie MacLaurin, Head of Sales at Birdie, was talking to some female colleagues at Birdie who said that they didn't feel supported if they were to have a child. And so, she took it to the founders.

> *"What we had was an equal parental leave policy where primary and secondary caregivers would get three months of paid leave. What I said to our founders was, 'Look, we've got 25% female representation in our leadership team, and the policy that we have for parental leave is incredibly generous for men, but it's bang average for women. And so my question is, who are we trying to attract? Because at the moment we've got a shortage of women and leadership and the maternity policies are not appealing or attractive enough.*
> *That was actually a penny-drop moment for them, because they do genuinely want a more diverse workforce. So they said, 'Great, can you think about what you would recommend?' We recommended six months parental leave for primary caregivers, three months for secondary."*

Organizations can make changes to craft a maternity policy that works, they often just need someone to kickstart it – we have more guidelines on this in Part Three. What all parties involved need to keep in mind, though, is that what works for one person might not work for another, and so the more candid and informed you are when going to your manager about what you need, the more likely you will be to get something that suits you. As part of this conversation there should also be a willingness to have good notes on all your clients as well as a collaborative approach from your manager/team to look after the clients, minimize impact, and increase chances of success.

APPROACHING A PROMOTION

When it comes to seeking a promotion, you should be bold and go for the role, even if you have doubts about whether you meet 100% of the requirements. Look beyond that to the key attributes – there's a likelihood that though you might think you meet 60% of the key attributes, it could actually be closer to 80-90%.

Before you do anything else to seek a promotion, research should be your top priority. What does the role require? Are there things you need to learn or achieve before you're ready to make that next step? This will help identify what your next steps should be.

Don't be afraid to be ambitious – this is where your plan comes in, you will have formulated an idea of what you want to achieve in the near and long term. Part of the next steps to do that is to have key conversations with your leader, a mentor or coach. We will elaborate on the role of a mentor or coach in the next chapter, but working alongside them can assist you in building out a plan to a promotion. If there is no annual performance planning or formal personal development process in your company, you can be proactive in the 1 to 1s with your line manager. Use these conversations to explore your next career step, identify key development areas, and gain clarity on the skills you need to build over the year. Regular feedback will help keep you on track and ensure you're continuously growing toward your goals.

MARINA: *Your career goals and ambitions should be a constant conversation, at the end of the day no one else owns your goals or development. They're not something that you have to make a meeting about, but rather something that you set as a goal and then in every one-to-one, it's about working on the development areas you've agreed. Making your leadership aware of your goals* *is so important to ensure everyone is on the same page, saying, "Marina, as you know, my real goal is to move into the Majors team and ideally I'd like to do that in the next 12 months. What would you need to see over the next 12 months to feel comfortable if there is a spot or an opening upcoming to put me in that role?" And then you can build a trackable plan together with some metrics around it to measure it.*

Use data to demonstrate what you've achieved and what more you could do should you get the promotion. Explain what it is about you that matches you for it, looking at your skills and attributes. Make it clear that you have thought about it – outline a plan about what you would do in the first 30/60/90 days.

Some of us have the idea that if we work hard enough, we will never need to ask for a promotion. But sometimes, if you don't make it known that you want something, no one will think to give it to you. If you think you're ready for that promotion – reach for it!

PENNY: *As a leader I ensure that personal and professional development of the members of my team is an ongoing part of their 1-1 cadence with me. That being said, it's important that the planning and preparation comes from the individual as well. When I have approached my conversations in regards to getting more additional responsibility I have been fully prepared with what I want to ask for and approach the conversation through the lens of how that will benefit the company.*

NEGOTIATING A PAY RISE OR STOCK

The first step to receiving a pay rise is, of course, to earn it. Work hard and demonstrate your value to your leader and your team. If you are aiming for a pay rise, it is useful to be familiar with the general policy and process of your company. Large companies tend to have pay bands in place to ensure there is equitable pay across their organization. Sales is split between a base and commission structure: combined gives the total OTE package. When looking for a pay rise on your salary the first thing a manager will look for is consistency in hitting or exceeding your targets. Consistently over-achieving will create a strong argument for an increase in your base. Some companies also have benchmarks based on experience and tenure, and there can also be an annual increase based on inflation. It is best to check these with HR if you do not know already. As you move up the ladder, other factors will come into play with regards to the increase of pay, including upcoming funding or investment that requires a need to reach a higher ARR number, or taking on a much bigger team, for example.

SOME TIPS WHEN LOOKING AT A PAY REVIEW:

- Do some research externally. What are peers getting paid in similar companies with similar targets?

- What proof points do you have that show you deserve it?

- Be professional, realistic and specific when asking for the additional compensation. What are you looking for?

Approaching a pay rise is not too far off from negotiating a price with a prospect. Focus on value, what you will deliver, how what you are asking for compares to what is being offered in the market, and suggest options: increased OTE with a higher base but some may be made up of equity, or it might be a blend of salary increase, bonus and stock based on output.

Like a promotion, if you don't ask for something, you won't get it. When you know it's right, be bold, and ask for that pay rise. You can be certain your colleagues will be!

ANNIE ANONYMOUS: *I feel that my male team members act entitled when it comes to pay cycles, as they genuinely believe that they are the best, and have performed well even when they have not. The way they approach pay increases and stock is totally different to the women within my teams. Women will come with data points and a request as to what they are looking for. The men are totally unrealistic and sometimes arrogant.*

I had an example where one of my team did not agree with the RSUs given as part of a promotion and wanted to decline the grant... It took 3 hours of explaining over and over that there would be no additional increase and it was not a negotiation before he accepted it.

Things to avoid doing when asking for a pay rise is to ask because you have been "headhunted for a great opportunity" or you have been "working long hours and deserve it". It's not about what you are owed, but rather, what you have earned.

PENNY: *It's ironic that I feel more comfortable negotiating with customers or on behalf of my team than I do for myself. That said, I try to push that aside and focus on my performance and what is fair when entering into pay discussions. In the past when I have asked for a pay increase I will start by researching into benchmarking my pay within my network (there are also places like Pavillion that have benchmarking data). This will look at the balance of equity/remuneration guarantees/paybacks – which are particularly important if going into a sales leadership role. Three things to keep in mind are: a) provide your manager some well thought through options b) tie clear performance metrics into any additions to your traditional comp plan (so there is an upside* *for both parties), c) make it a no-brainer (provide historical performance data, your pipeline, and indicators on how this will improve growth for the business).*

There are certain constants to keep in mind for every crucial conversation. First, research is king. You can never be over-prepared, or have too much information. So dive into research before starting a discussion on something that you hope to gain. Second, confidence is a game-changer. This confidence can come from yourself, from the internal ability to be bold and take a leap of faith, or it can come from the support of those around you.

These conversations are important to your career development, but there is no reason to be afraid of them. Your leaders want you to progress and they want you to succeed, just like you do.

Chapter 7: Crucial Conversations

Whether discussing parental leave, asking for a promotion, or negotiating a pay rise, thorough research and preparation are crucial. Understanding company policies, knowing your performance metrics, and being aware of industry standards help you approach these conversations with confidence and clarity.

Don't wait for opportunities to come to you—take charge of your career by initiating conversations about your goals. Being direct and confident about your needs is key to advancing your career.

Each conversation requires a different strategy. Be informed, present compelling data about your achievements, and, when applicable, offer multiple options that benefit both you and the organization. Flexibility and open communication increase the likelihood of finding mutually agreeable solutions.

Chapter Eight

MENTORS, COACHES, AND CHAMPIONS

Whether it's a mentor, coach or champion, each of them are instrumental in helping you accelerate and drive your career forward. There is a difference between the three – which we will cover shortly – but regardless of which, having the right person will be hugely beneficial. They can be the trusted person you turn to when you need help solving more tangible problems, like, "I don't know what to do in this deal," or issues with a manager or colleague as well as when you feel stuck in your career.

Research has proven that mentoring is beneficial, both when it comes to job satisfaction and earning potential.[66] Not only that, but it has also been found that salespeople with mentors perform better both in the short and long term.[67] When engaged with correctly, mentors can propel you and your career forward with much-needed advice and a guiding hand. During our research it was clear that having a good mentor has been instrumental to the success of many in their rise to sales leadership. In the event that there are not as many women in leadership roles, providing them with strong mentors is important.

FROM MELISSA DI DONATO, CEO AND CHAIR AT KYRIBA:

A thing we need to do to keep women in sales and push them to success is to put them in touch with other role models and mentors. My whole life has been driven by mentors, even at my age and at my position, I still call my mentor.

MENTOR, COACH OR CHAMPION?

A mentor is usually someone more senior to you and in a role that you aspire to, or has more experience than you in your current role. A mentor is not to be confused with a coach or a champion. A champion, sometimes referred to as a sponsor, plays a critical role in career advancement, particularly at senior levels. Unlike a mentor, who primarily offers advice and support, a champion actively advocates for you, ensuring your name is in the conversation for key opportunities, promotions, or high-profile projects. Champions are typically senior leaders with influence, using their credibility to open doors you may not have access to on your own. While a mentor can also be a champion, the distinction lies in action – mentors guide, while champions push for your advancement. Having a champion is often a crucial factor in breaking into leadership roles.

Another person that can be of value as you seek to advance your career is a career coach. They are usually professionally retained, and charge for their time. A coach might not have direct experience in your field like a mentor would, but they will have certain expertise that they can impart to you. The return on investment for a career coach is likely to be financial, while for a mentor it is more of a mutual exchange of value. The structure of coaching will likely come from the coach, while in mentorship the mentee is more responsible for the agenda. Coaches and mentors can help you achieve your career goals, and both can be instrumental in your success, while you might lean on them at different points.

Mentor	I Senior to you I Provides advice and coaching I Typically in a role you aspire to I Mentee typically responsible for the agenda
Champion	I Often, but not always, senior to you I Solid reputation I Advocates for you when you're not in the room, recommending you for roles and promotions
Coach	I Charge for their time I May not have direct field experience, but will have otherwise useful expertise I Tends to lead the structure of coaching
Buddy	I Peers I Within your team or another team in your organization I Typically more tenured than you I Serves as an informal and friendly resource for newcomers to a team or company

PENNY: *I have had mentors and coaches at various stages of my career, and would strongly advise anyone reading this to get one too. If you get the right one, and invest in them, they will be critical to your success. Usually I work with someone who is an expert in the role I am new to or want, and/or a coach who works with me on communication, positive mindset, leadership skills, and change management. I have had both female and male mentors as I believe it's really important to get different perspectives.*

MENTORS AND HOW TO FIND THEM

Finding the right mentor for you can largely depend on personal preference – what do you want from the mentorship? What stage in your career are you? How would your ideal mentor help you achieve your goals? These are the questions you should ask yourself before looking for a mentor, but here are some best practices to keep in mind when seeking mentorship.

1. Find someone whose experience is relevant to the role you are aspiring to and your sector. That can be someone who's in the same role as you but more experienced, someone who has been successful in your role in the past, or someone who is in a role you aspire to.

2. Think about it from a practical standpoint: what do you want to get better at? Who do you see excelling at that thing? That is the kind of person you should approach. You can also factor in what you want to achieve, and how exactly someone could help you with that.

3. Look at people who have done mentoring before. Some people will have information in their LinkedIn profile that can indicate that mentorship is something they care about. There are also many sales communities that you can join, whether you are an SDR, AE or a manager, that you can leverage to find a mentor.

4. Tap into your network. Ask people – including your manager – if they can recommend a mentor.

5. Create compelling messaging when you reach out. Through a well thought out message or video you should be able to articulate why you want this person as your mentor, and why they should mentor you.

When seeking out potential mentors, it's also good to keep in mind the benefit that comes with a variety of perspectives on your career. If you are a woman in sales looking to progress, hearing from a successful female sales leader can be very advantageous. That being said, gender-matched mentoring is not necessarily the only way to do it. There could be a plethora of expertise that you miss because you go for a mentor of your own gender. The knowledge possessed by a female sales leader is just as applicable to an aspiring male salesperson as his female counterpart, and the same is true vice versa. Expertise isn't based solely on gender, after all. If you have a blend of mentors, career champions, and a diverse selection of perspectives on your career, you ensure your professional education is well-rounded.

MELISSA DI DONATO, CEO AND CHAIR AT KYRIBA, ON MIXED MENTORSHIP:

Every male and female salesperson should absolutely have female and male mentors. Women only give you a certain percentage of the perspective; they're not necessarily going to experience the same things and same hardships. In fact, some of the problems I have, men are not immune to; it's the same issues in different clothing. I also highly encourage different industries and different backgrounds – you don't just want people with the same background as you.

ENSURING A MUTUAL EXCHANGE OF VALUE

Mentoring is a two-way street. A mentor is giving up their valuable time to help you, and so you need to be respectful of that time and the expertise they are offering you by making that time count. There is no point in approaching someone you admire and saying, "I think mentorship is great, I'd love to get an hour of your time," only for your mentor to spend that time and then for everything to cease. You can add to the value of your mentorship by building a mutually beneficial relationship that includes exchanging ideas, energy, and insight into other areas of an organization or industry.

To be mindful of your mentor's time, you need to do thorough preparation before each session with them. Ahead of your first call this is especially important: be proactive and do the research into what you want to learn and what your mentor could share with you. When you know what you are looking for and why they can help, you cement the relationship's success. Think: what draws you to them, and why do you want them to be your mentor? Maybe more importantly, why should they want to work with you?

To continue to make the mentorship worthwhile, make sure you action the suggestions they give you in between sessions, and work with them to look at outcomes for each session, as they will want to see the impact of their guidance. For your mentor, satisfaction will ultimately come from confirmation that what they are doing is meaningful and helping you in your career.

A NOTE FROM ANDY WHYTE, CEO AT MEDDICC:

One of the biggest challenges with mentorship is that highly successful people – those most sought after as mentors – are often time-poor. Add to that the fact that the main reward for mentoring is personal satisfaction, which isn't always tangible, and you have a tricky situation where mentors lack both time and motivation.

I saw this firsthand when Alex Miller, then an SDR and daughter of the late sales trainer Skip Miller, reached out. She wanted to build a career in sales enablement, but at the moment she needed her father's mentorship most, he wasn't there. Seeking guidance from other mentors, she faced the same challenge – busy professionals with limited availability.

> *To solve this, I suggested a different approach: instead of just asking for mentorship, offer value in return. Alex launched the Skip to the Point podcast, where she interviews experts she admires, amplifying their insights while gaining mentorship herself. This strategy creates a win-win: mentees gain knowledge, while mentors see their wisdom shared widely. If you're looking for mentorship in sales, tuning into Skip to the Point is a great place to start!*

PENNY: *With my mentor, there are a few things I do to make sure the time we spend together is valuable. The first is that I always turn up on time and ensure we have a consistent cadence of when we meet. The second is that I prepare. For each call I will have a list of questions that I ask them. Each session has follow up actions based on the advice that we reconnect on in the next session. I am respectful of their time and advice and invest fully in the process so it's not a waste of their time or mine.*

AS SAID BY RONAL KARIA, VP OF SALES (CENTRAL AND NORTHERN EUROPE) AT SLACK:

> *I mentor a number of people, both internally and externally, and in the first conversation I have when they approach me, I go, "What is it you want out of this mentorship?" Then, every session we finish, I sort of summarize and give them things to go and do. Not to say my time is more important than theirs, but I want them to go and take action or think about certain things for the next session because, like with everything, you get busy and you forget about it. You come up to the next session, and you go, "What did we talk about last time?" and that means you've done nothing with it. Mentorship is only valuable if you put the time and effort into it as a mentee and learn from it and take actions from it.*

HOW TO STRUCTURE YOUR MENTORSHIP

While interactions with career coaches are often used to exchange ideas and receive advice, a mentorship thrives with structure – with a formal plan and an agenda.

MENTORSHIP STRUCTURE

1 **Purpose, build rapport and set the tone**

Catch up

Set objectives

2 **Dive into specific issues/challenges you face and/or goals of session or mentorship**

3 **Skills and Development. What are you hoping to achieve to drive growth and career advancement?**

4 **Scenario Practice. Apply what you are trying to learn into a live scenario – role play perhaps – if that is asking for a pay rise, how do you go about this?**

5 **Q&A**

6 **Close, summarize and plan next steps**

Once you have mutually agreed the mentorship is beneficial for both parties, here is an example of how you can create structured mentorship discussions:

MENTORING MISTAKES

As a potential mentee, it can be disheartening when your dream mentor turns you down. It can be equally frustrating for both parties if you emerge from a mentorship and realize you haven't learned or achieved anything. But why would this happen? Here are some faux pas to keep in mind when pursuing a mentorship.

Panacea Treatment

Something that can take the wind out of a mentorship's sails before it's even on the water is when people treat it like a cure for all ills. Without knowing where they need to improve, or with what they're even looking for help, some people will seek out a mentor because they heard it was good to have one. As a result, they don't know who to approach, or what kind of guidance they might need. What follows is one of two things. The first is that they approach the wrong person – maybe someone who doesn't have the right level of experience, or who hasn't experienced the issues that you are looking to be coached on. As a result, they can't help you. The second thing that happens is that if they do get the ear of their perfect mentor, they don't know how to really get value from their time, because they don't know what to ask for. In either situation, the prospective mentee wastes their own time and that of their potential mentor.

Checking the Box

Another obstacle to a mentorship is when the mentee treats it like a tick-box exercise. Maybe they heard or read somewhere that having a mentor is the key to getting ahead in their industry, so they seek someone out in order to say, "Oh yeah, that person is my mentor." But when you do this without the real intent of learning something, and fostering a mutually beneficial relationship with a mentor, your insincerity is palpable. More importantly, little is gained from the partnership. Once again, you would be wasting your time, and that of someone who has been gracious enough to spend their valuable time with you. If a mentee doesn't have skin in the game, the mentor can be left feeling unappreciated and frustrated because they have given their valuable time to someone who didn't recognize the worth of what they were sharing.

LUCY: *I did some mentoring a while ago… Well, more like I agreed to do some mentoring; when I met with the mentees, they showed up with no questions, agenda, or thought. Afterwards, they did not follow up or even say thank you. It was a total waste of time! I think if the person who approached me to do it had coached the mentee a little better in the first place it would have been mutually valuable but in this instance, I really believe it was a true tick-box exercise and it ended up being a waste of time for both parties.*

WE ASKED RONAL KARIA, VP OF SALES (CENTRAL AND NORTHERN EUROPE), ABOUT MISTAKES PEOPLE MAKE WHEN PURSUING MENTORSHIP:

Going for people they like! I get that you don't want someone you hate to be a mentor, because you need to have a conversation, but don't just go, "I admire that person, so I want them to be a mentor," or "They're really like me," or "I want to be like them," actually think back to what you want out of a mentor and what you want from them. Then, go and try to find somebody who has those skills, who has been through that journey, rather than just going for the first person that somebody suggests because they're successful. Just because they're successful doesn't mean they're going to make you successful because actually, mentorship is about you, not them.

When you put in the effort with your mentor, you will see the reward. And remember, a mentor is not necessarily forever. Often, they serve a purpose for a moment of time on a journey. So make sure to do what you can to get the most from the time spent with your mentor, and when you have attained the knowledge and expertise you aimed for, don't hesitate to pay it forward!

PENNY: *My mentorships have usually changed or ended for a couple of reasons.*
1. I've either changed role or company, and so require something different
2. I feel like I have got to a good place with the new learnings and so take a break.

It is perfectly natural for a mentorship to end at some point, and it can even reignite a few years later.

Something else to keep in mind is that your ideal mentor might not even be a mentor – or at least, not in an official capacity. Feel free to look for unofficial channels of mentoring where you have identified room for improvement. There may be people around you who inspire you and whose advice you trust – like friends or family – who are in a way an informal mentorship channel. In addition if you have a gap in your development and you see someone in that area (in or out of your organization!) that excels at what they do, there is nothing to be lost from reaching out. This way, you can build a good relationship that can teach you a lot, without the potential demand on time that could come with a traditional mentorship.

MARINA: *Mentoring for me is more than just training; it's about paving the way for the next generation of sales leaders. I love working with young up and coming talents who are earlier in their careers, creating a system where my knowledge and best practices can be shared. I think it's really important as female sales leaders to share our wisdom, guiding mentees through challenges, celebrating successes, and helping them to believe in themselves and unlock their full potential. In return, as a mentor I find I can gain fresh perspectives, learn new skills (especially in AI and automation) which actually helps me stay relevant!*

Chapter 8: Mentors, Coaches, and Champions

Mentors, coaches, and champions each play distinct but crucial roles in career advancement. Mentors provide guidance and advice based on their experience, coaches offer structured professional expertise, and champions advocate for you in your absence. For women in sales leadership, mentorship is particularly critical, offering role models and tailored support to help navigate challenges.

A successful mentorship hinges on a clear understanding of goals and mutual value. Mentees must prepare for sessions, articulate their objectives, follow through on advice, and maintain respect for their mentor's time. This structured approach ensures productive, meaningful interactions that benefit both parties.

Missteps in pursuing mentorship include treating it as a universal solution without clear goals or selecting a mentor based solely on admiration rather than relevant expertise. Another frequent issue is a lack of commitment, where mentees fail to engage thoughtfully, undermining the relationship's value. Successful mentorship demands effort, alignment, and intentionality.

PART THREE

HOW ORGANIZATIONS CAN ATTRACT AND PROMOTE MORE *WOMEN IN SALES*

When we set out to write this book, we did so with the specific goal of getting more women into senior sales leadership positions, in large part because we know the positive impact diversity has on teams and organizations. The diversity of thought that comes from a team filled with all kinds of people, each with unique life experiences and perspectives, brings benefits that we have seen firsthand. Not only that, but studies have shown that organizations with diverse leadership teams outperform their less diverse counterparts – a 2015 McKinsey study found that in the UK, for every 10% increase in gender diversity on the senior-executive team, EBIT [Earning Before Interest and Taxes] increased by 3.5%.[68]

In Part One, we explored why women should pursue tech sales, highlighting its innovation, financial independence, and career variety. We discussed the skills that help women succeed, the challenges of a male-dominated industry, and the opportunities available – sharing stories to illustrate both the obstacles and the potential for growth.

In Part Two we hoped to demonstrate through the experiences of ourselves and the contributors options available to you for career progression in sales, and practical steps you can take to be successful.

A crucial piece of the puzzle in increasing the number of women in senior sales leadership is the role that organizations and leaders play in attracting and advancing female talent. People don't tend to succeed in isolation; pretty much everyone who has achieved anything has done so with support from those around them. If we want more women to succeed in sales and sales leadership, it's imperative that software sales organizations support and advocate for women. This can be done at an individual level of allyship, but it also needs to happen on a larger scale. In Part Three, we are looking at what organizations can do to not only attract more women to sales, but also retain and promote through the right policies, culture and environment. We will talk about what organizations can do to build more diverse teams, as well as why they should do it in the first place. Part of that comes down to more balanced hiring practices. There are a number of practical steps that organizations and leaders can take to build an environment that is inclusive for all, beyond just policies, that we have seen in our careers and will share with you here.

We hope that this helps to drive impact through wider support.

Chapter Nine

BUILDING A DIVERSE TEAM

We have already touched on the benefits of building a diverse team, many of which you likely would have guessed already. It makes it possible for people from all walks of life to enter the world of tech sales, and diversity of background leads to diversity of thought, which can only be a good thing. In addition the data also shows that gender and general diversity has a positive impact on team and company performance.

The numbers don't lie: the more diverse your leadership team, as we hinted earlier, the better your organization will perform. A 2016 analysis of over 20,000 firms across 91 countries found that businesses with a higher number of female executives tended to be more profitable.[69] This trend continues: a 2023 McKinsey study found that companies in the top quartile of representation of women on executive teams are 39% more likely to be profitable than the average.[70] Conversely, companies with low rates of gender diversity are more likely to lag behind the average when it comes to profitability.[71]

This is great news – but why does it happen?

Studies have found that "deep-level diversity" is linked to greater team innovation.[72] This is the case even in the realm of science, where it has been discovered that mixed-gender teams "produce more novel and more highly cited papers" than single-gender teams.[73] You might wonder why this is the case, or why is there a difference at all? While at first it might come as a surprise, it does make sense. With a collection of unique perspectives, you allow for increased creativity as everyone is encouraged to consider situations in different lights, which breeds a wider variety of approaches and solutions. It has also been found that diversity increases employee satisfaction, collaboration and loyalty.[74] Happier salespeople are much more likely to be successful salespeople, as they approach every deal with optimism and a hard-working attitude.

KATHRYN POOL, SENIOR DIRECTOR, HEAD OF ENTERPRISE RETAIL INDUSTRY AT MICROSOFT UK:

I think, as women, we bring that diversity of opinion, we have empathy and we approach things differently because we have a different set of eyes. I have a diverse team, about a 50:50 ratio, and I just think we bring so much more to the table than all male teams.

On top of that, a focus on a more gender diverse company can assist companies who are struggling to find the right salespeople. Some venture capitalists and companies are focusing on partnerships with organizations that support women entrepreneurs and leaders, such as women-focused networking events or investment groups, to ensure a broader pool of candidates. Such funds include Angel Academe and January Ventures. Sometimes an issue can lie in what organizations consider the 'right' salesperson. Not only does it make strategic sense for companies to extend talent searches for women (and other marginalized groups), it increases the pool of candidates, providing access to a wider range of skills, perspectives, and experiences. When skill shortages are a top reason for vacancies, looking outside of your 'typical' talent pool can make it easier to find the perfect person for the role.[75] This approach helps build a more balanced workload, allowing your team to focus on their core responsibilities and excel. Everyone wins!

LAURA LENTI, VP EMEA AT NEPTUNE SOFTWARE:

> *I've hired some women since I've been in leadership who haven't had the typical track record in getting into sales and I've seen the impact they make; how it changes the culture, and encourages everyone to have fun and spar with different ideas. Having that difference in perspective and experience, when you're with people who aren't like you, it helps everyone to grow.*

BUILDING AND DRIVING AN ENVIRONMENT THAT FOSTERS INCLUSIVITY

An integral component of building a diverse team is creating an environment where diversity is celebrated. But that isn't something that happens overnight – it takes conscious work, and it starts at the leadership level. Here are some tips for how leaders, HR, and organizations overall can support managers to build and grow a diverse team.

1. Establish defined KPIs on an Exec level that support Diversity and Inclusion (D&I) and drive forward the company values, e.g. targets on diversity in hiring or the company's Employee Net Promoter Score.

2. Review hiring processes to remove gender bias. We go in depth on how you can do this in chapter 10, but it includes

training hiring managers, expanding your hiring network and rethinking how performance is evaluated.

3. Support and help improve the manager/employee relationship by training managers on how to effectively coach and building manager awareness of the experience of underrepresented groups.

4. Create networks and communities internally, with active participation from leadership. Gartner research shows that organizations implementing networking programs for underrepresented talent are twice as likely to be seen by HR leaders as successful in fostering inclusion and 1.3 times more likely to be effective in boosting engagement among diverse employees.[76]

5. Highlight successful women within the organization or industry. This can inspire other women and demonstrate that leadership roles are attainable. Companies can host speaking engagements or panel discussions featuring female executives.

Creating a Culture Built on Trust and Respect

Fostering inclusion in your work environment is not something accomplished by ticking boxes on a checklist – rather it is about establishing a culture where everyone feels safe, one built on trust and respect. We've talked about how important trust is to a team, because it allows people to feel able to take risks and to grow.

Trust within a team is often driven by an environment of psychological safety. That means people "feel safe to take interpersonal risks, to speak up, to disagree openly, to surface concerns without fear of negative repercussions or pressure to sugarcoat bad news." According to one McKinsey survey, 89% of respondents said they believe that psychological safety in the workplace is essential.[77]

Not only do employees view an environment with psychological safety as essential, but it is where the highest performing teams operate. As found by McKinsey, psychological safety "contributes to team effectiveness, learning, employee retention, and – most critically – better decisions and better performance."[78]

When a leader focuses on creating an environment where their team feels comfortable, with a focus on psychological safety, it builds trust. It says that the leader has their back, which allows the team to be vulnerable. When this happens, people are open to taking risks, acknowledging when they need help, and feel comfortable asking for that help. All of which speeds up learning, progression and overall team performance.

A way to foster psychological safety in teams is with consultative leadership. By consulting team members, seeking their input and genuinely taking their perspective into consideration, it tells the team that you trust their input, which prompts them to trust you too.

Listening and ensuring everyone has a voice is instrumental in initiating trust in your team. Welcome being challenged, and keep an open mind as you hear differing opinions. Diverse teams thrive because they bring diversity of thought, but only if that diversity of thought is embraced.

That goes both ways. As a leader, you owe it to your team to respect them when you give them feedback. Open communication and transparency is so important, and sharing your intentions early on is key.

AS SAID BY KATHRYN POOL:

It's important to give everyone the opportunity to speak. In any team, male, female, or whatever, there's always an element of the

> *introverts who feel less confident. So, what I say is, "For those of you who haven't said anything, is there something you'd like to contribute?" or, "For anyone who hasn't yet spoken, do they want to share their opinions?"*

AS SAID BY JOSH REINER, VP EMEA AT WIZ:

> *Trust is earned in drops and lost in buckets. If you don't go out of your way to build a diverse culture, you won't. If you want to be proud of where you work, you need to build that culture. It doesn't happen by chance.*

LUCY: *In the first team meeting of the year, I always set out the team mantra and the core principles I would like to adopt across the team. These are not just my ideas, but come from constant feedback from the team as to an environment they would like to work and thrive within. Open, respectful, transparent communication is always one of these.. When building the team culture, I want to ensure everyone feels able to speak up, share their views and trust one another to have their backs. Teams who adopt this approach are often more performant than others*

When a team trusts and respects each other, it makes it easier to call out bad behavior.

BUILDING A POSITIVE CULTURE AND ENSURING INCLUSION

When you establish an environment where people from different backgrounds and walks of life can thrive, you will attract a diverse range of candidates and employees. When you have more women in your team, for example, they are more likely to bring in and hire other women, which boosts the gender balance in your team. When you don't address the issues that hold a team back from embracing diversity, it can be detrimental to anyone's confidence and self esteem.

ANNIE ANONYMOUS: *I heard a story about someone who was already attending therapy for his stutter who was asked to participate in a role play in front of a full room of people. He was clearly nervous, but did it with his voice shaking a bit. The leader said, "Do it again, but without the stutter." This kind of leadership not only undermines the individual but also fosters a toxic culture where unacceptable behavior is normalized.*

But how do you establish a more inclusive sales team on a broader scale?

Driven from the Top Down

Change is most effective when it starts at the top. A 2019 report from Catalyst discovered that a manager practicing inclusive leadership led to 45% of employee experiences of inclusion.[79] Additionally, having a manager who really cares about their well-being is one of the top three factors women tend to consider when it comes to joining or staying at a company.[80] As touched on when we discussed allyship, when leaders get involved in an initiative, they demonstrate to the entire team its importance.

PENNY: *Meaningful change starts at the top, but it only truly takes hold when it's embedded across the entire business. For gender diversity to improve, it must be a CEO-level priority – driven with intention, backed by clear targets, and supported by a structured program. When it's part of the Exec and Board OKRs, with accountability in place, progress happens. But without the CEO's commitment, in my experience, the impact is minimal.*

At SUSE, I worked under my first female CEO, Melissa Di Donato. Anyone who knows her knows she is a strong advocate for women. She didn't just 'talk the talk' – she 'walked the walk,' challenging the status quo and deeply understanding the obstacles women face on the path to leadership. During her tenure, she prioritized DEI policies, and almost 50% of her Exec team were women, with some of the strongest diversity I have seen across the whole organization in my career. It was also the first leadership offsite where I witnessed the Exec dancing to ABBA in feather boas and hats! It was a truly unique culture.

This is also why it's so necessary to have women in sales leadership positions. Research has shown that women in leadership go beyond their male counterparts in promoting employee well-being and advancing diversity, equity, and inclusion.[81] Women play a pivotal role in creating a more inclusive workplace.

On top of that, if new female starters enter and see women in senior positions, they are shown a path to that level. While many are certainly capable of forging their own path, having someone lead the way can be majorly impactful and of course, inspiring. Executives are increasingly recognizing the importance of mentorship and sponsorship for women in the workplace. Initiatives that pair women with experienced leaders help provide guidance, support, and opportunities for career advancement.

MARINA: *Having female leaders is crucial for inspiring the next generation of leaders and demonstrating what is possible. It allows us to pave the way for others to strive for more, even when it challenges the norm. Having women in leadership positions is also powerful from a recruitment perspective; having women in leadership roles makes it significantly easier to attract female talent. In my current position at WIZ, we have two senior female leaders in the UK, which has allowed us to achieve an impressive near 50/50 gender split in our sales team. This balance is not only amazing but essential for fostering diverse perspectives and driving success.*

Female leaders can set standards for how they are to be treated that will filter through the organization, which will then attract more women to the company; advancing in their careers would be more appealing to two-thirds of women under 30 if they saw senior leaders with the work-life balance they want.[82] When there is a female presence in an organization's leadership team, it signals to the whole team and to the outside how important women are to them and the degree of respect that they are afforded by this organization.

However, it's important that the organization doesn't let the full weight of this lie with the woman. Otherwise it can lead to an unfair extra amount of responsibilities that could lead to burn out.

AS SAID BY KATHRYN POOL:

When I started out, I was one of the only salespeople in the room who was female. When you have a woman on your team, especially in leadership, diversity breeds diversity. As women we tend to bring more women into the team. Not many women have worked under a female leader and I think they're curious. I think it should be widely encouraged.

Another important element of driving inclusion from the top down comes with implementing formal unconscious bias training. Statistics show that education on how we may be affected by our unconscious biases can make real change; a 2017 study across selected STEMM departments at a specific university found that the departments that made an effort to 'intervene' in unconscious bias hired 18% more female faculty after the intervention.[83] When leaders put this kind of training into action, it creates a lasting effect on the entire organization.

PENNY: *When I worked at Meta, they had mandatory unconscious bias training as part of their onboarding programme in week one. They developed their materials internally, collaborating with external experts on their internal online HR platform and it was truly excellent! DEI was also noted as a key pillar for the company in Sheryl Sandberg's (COO) recorded introduction talk to the company. So as a new employee it very much set the tone, and I knew it was a key pillar to the company DNA.*

FIONA MCCLUNE, CRO AT STRUCTUREFLOW, ON ENCOURAGING MORE WOMEN INTO SALES LEADERSHIP:

I think this is a multifaceted approach, but it's about promoting diversity and inclusion through culture, and having that at the front and foremost of an organization. Fostering an environment where everyone's voices are heard equally, and not only that, that they're also respected. From a practical point of view, understanding why diverse perspectives are valued, it's about implementing mentorship programs and creating leadership development programs that are targeted at female talent.

Active Inclusivity

A sense of inclusion is a key factor in employee satisfaction and retention. Often, the absence of inclusion isn't intentional. Without knowing, the way we communicate and interact with a team or one-on-one with someone can make certain team members, like women, feel unwelcome in a space. Consider team-building events, for example. Default activities like going for drinks or organizing rounds of golf might be fun ways to get to know your colleagues, relying solely on those means you are only getting to know a certain group of people.

ANNIE ANONYMOUS: *Recently, there was a golf day organized for customers and some of the internal sales ecosystem. As organization began, only the men in my team were made aware of it and invited to be involved. I have a woman in my team who is incredible at golf, with a lower handicap than many of the men, but she was excluded and only found out about it by accident. Exclusion due to perception, based on gender is not okay. The same goes for when there are football or rugby events, it's the same people attending, time and time again. This needs to change.*

By failing to have a variety of team-building events, you could be unknowingly excluding so many different people. This extends past just women; think of someone who doesn't drink for religious reasons – they might not want to go to the pub every Friday, but may feel uncomfortable suggesting alternatives. When you make more of an effort to be inclusive, you welcome people from all walks of life. You might not think inclusive team-building activities are that necessary, but failing to include women in them can hinder them professionally; over a third of women report missing professional opportunities because discussions occurred outside the workplace.[84]

Leaders can also introduce education and training to promote inclusive behaviors in the workplace. Not only will this make the workplace more welcoming for women, but it will also help the entire workforce to be more considerate of one another and improve general morale. One way to foster inclusivity is by establishing a social committee composed of diverse individuals who plan events that cater to different interests, beliefs, and perspectives. To ensure engagement, employees can participate in voting on activities or contribute their own ideas for team-building events. This not only makes social initiatives more meaningful but also strengthens workplace connections and collaboration.

Creating Internal Community

As a woman in sales, it can sometimes feel isolating. You can look around you, and it may seem that no one else, including the other women in your organization, are experiencing any degree of difficulty; that the struggles in your path affect you and you alone. But when you do a little digging, you'll find that isn't the case. In fact, it is incredibly likely that problems you are facing affect other women as well.

MELISSA DI DONATO, CEO AND CHAIR AT KYRIBA, ON THE IMPORTANCE OF COMMUNITY:

It's really simple, but I think the 'birds of a feather flock together' thing is really important for women. Women need other women as mentors, as role models, as sounding boards. At a previous organization]we used to do a lunch for all the female salespeople for us to sit around and laugh, talk, and even complain or moan, or do whatever we wanted to do. It was a warm, safe environment for you to be natural in who you are and to be able to discuss the issues and the hardships that you're facing.

To overcome that sense of isolation, and to help yourself and other women in your organization, you can create a female community guild or group, where you can all support one another. You can share common struggles, and work to surmount them. Perhaps more importantly, you can use this group to lift one another up, and empower each other to succeed in the sales world.

Leaders can support the women in their organization in developing these communities by giving them the autonomy to create these internal groups or communities where they can connect and build that supportive environment.

MARINA: *At Zscaler, we held monthly breakfasts aimed at bringing together women from all levels of the organization, fostering a strong sense of camaraderie among us. I've found that inviting women who are interviewing with us to these gatherings is particularly beneficial, as it exemplifies our commitment to community and demonstrates that our focus extends beyond merely meeting a diversity quota.*

PENNY: *There have been Women In Tech (WiT) ERGs in the last 2 companies I have worked at – the more recent one I lead. WiT at SUSE was well established with an annual budget, and a commitment on deliverables to the Executive team lead by the Committee and Executive Sponsor. Through their string operating model they policy changes, a series of educational talks and a number networking events across the globe.*

Creating ERGs and networks is not only important to support the women in an organization and to build a community of like-mindedness but also to educate those around them. Including anyone who is interested in these groups prevents causing any division, and can educate and illuminate others as to the challenges that women face. It's essential that these groups remain open to all, as making them women-only could unintentionally create division rather than fostering inclusion.

AS SAID BY EMMA MULQUEENY OBE, HEAD OF ESG AT CAUSEWAY:

> *A Women in Tech ERG should be mandatory in every company to ensure it provides a space for people to come together and build a community, a group that can influence policy, maintain visibility with the Exec team, and serve as a collective voice. It should truly drive the 'S' in ESG.*

A Catalyst report suggested that men's involvement in discussion groups on gender, both male-only and mixed gender, can enhance their confidence and understanding of workplace gender issues.[85] It makes the subject of gender disparity less taboo, and encourages everyone to play a part in achieving gender equality.

LUCY: *When I joined Datadog we were very small, with less than 1000 employees, but as we have grown we have implemented Community Guilds to ensure there are safe spaces and a sense of community and belonging for all. Having a programme such as this in any mature company is so important, and should always form part of an organization's growth plans.*

I was fortunate enough to be asked to be the founding Co-Lead of the Women of Datadog, setting in place committees and workflows to ensure we had a successful first two years. The guilds act as a support network, amplifying diverse voices and ensuring that inclusion is not just a checkbox, but a core part of the organization's DNA. As well as Women of Datadog, we have guilds that represent a multitude of diversity and identities representing our employees.

Flexible Working

In Deloitte's Women in the Workplace study, it was found that for 62% of women, a more flexible schedule (including the ability to work from home) was their biggest motivation to succeed.[86] Flexibility is not about deprioritizing career ambitions – it allows women to perform at their best while managing responsibilities outside of work. Many highly ambitious women value the ability to structure their work in a way that maximizes productivity without rigid constraints.[87] This flexibility can include being considerate of when you do team meetings. Early morning meetings, for example, can be tricky for those with children to bring to school – so if they can be avoided, why not choose another time?

PENNY: *When I run my internal leadership weekly meetings I make sure they are held at times that can accommodate school runs or family commitments. To me it's really about productivity and output rather than micromanaging people's time. I have found the more flexible you are the greater the output and level of commitment. It's another way of showing respect and developing trust.*

To make a more inclusive environment for women in sales, making these accommodations, when you can, is essential. Most tech companies now have a hybrid working model, especially because you can access a much wider workforce when you don't need them to key cities and hubs where offices are, although there is more of a push recently to be in the office some days. Sometimes, of course, it isn't possible. The nature of sales means you might need to be in a different country to see a customer or prospect, or you might need to physically see your team for a QBR. When you have an established degree of trust and respect with your team, they will understand that flexibility can only extend so far. However, when you do make the effort to allow them to fit their work around their life, it shows them that the organization cares about their needs, and indeed their safety. Deloitte found that when women work at least partially remotely, they are less likely to experience microaggressions and tend to feel more psychologically safe.[88] This is especially true for women of underrepresented groups, be they women of color, LGBTQ+ or disabled women.[89] To ensure a truly welcoming culture for all women, leaders need to take more flexible work environments at least into consideration.

HOW DO YOU BUILD A DIVERSE TEAM?

- **Drive change from the top down: having allies and more women in leadership sets a standard that filters down through an organization**

- **Practice active inclusivity: you can talk the inclusive talk, but you need to walk the inclusive walk! Ensure team-building activities don't just appeal to one kind of person**

- **Introduce flexibility: while sales is a busy industry, maintaining a work-life balance is important for a better, happier team.**

The numbers and testimonies tell it like it is – a diverse team is a success-driver. A sales team with a range of lived experiences brings fresh perspectives to problems and can relate and appeal to a broader range of customers. Not only does it open the doors for people from all walks of life to enter the world of tech sales, it benefits the team and entire organization as a result.

Building a diverse team isn't a tick-box exercise; it takes work. But the results speak for themselves.

A NOTE FROM PETE CROSBY, FOUNDER AND CEO OF REVELSCO:

When the workplace is set up as a patriarchy, it makes it really difficult to get the best out of the women in our organization, which becomes self-defeating. If a woman is put in a position where she is set up to fail and then is blamed for failing – is that her fault or is that the fault of the infrastructure she's operating in? That's why I strongly believe that whether you're a woman, a black person, a black woman, a gay person, or whoever you might be, we need to create the conditions that allow you to succeed because you will succeed in areas that other people cannot.

Chapter 9: Building a Diverse Team

- Organizations with diverse leadership teams perform better financially and experience higher levels of creativity and collaboration, which drives both innovation and employee satisfaction.

- Leadership plays a key role in fostering inclusivity by setting measurable diversity goals, providing bias training, and creating an environment where all employees feel valued and supported.

- Women in leadership provide mentorship and visible career paths for others, while internal networks and flexible work options promote retention and a balanced, inclusive workplace.

- Addressing unconscious bias and promoting inclusive networks helps create lasting change by raising awareness, fostering accountability, and encouraging allyship across the organization.

- A diverse sales team brings unique perspectives that help companies connect with a broader customer base, leading to enhanced performance and long-term business success.

Chapter Ten

HIRING

When trying to analyze why there's a lack of women in sales and sales leadership, there's a few places you might go instinctually. Is it because of the workplace culture? Are women just less suited to sales? (Spoilers: it isn't either of those).

In fact, one reason can be traced right back to the root of your career journey; to the hiring practices. It goes without saying that there are some women who are never going to go for a career in sales, nevermind sales leadership. However, those who do have an interest, and could go on to be excellent salespeople and leaders, can be hindered before they even get in the door, if they get through the door at all.

Right now, the higher proportion of men in sales roles is the status quo. Part of what maintains the status quo is people's tendency to view and defend it as natural, or just how things should be.[90] In this context, it means that when some people look at the gender imbalance in sales, they think, "That's just how it's always been," so there is just a level of acceptance about it. If we don't make a conscious effort to highlight the importance of women coming into sales and sales leadership, the status quo and the perception of it will never change. This inequality is also kept afloat by "institutional-level mechanisms" – the structural systems and processes that keep an institution, or an organization, running. If we don't examine how organization-wide processes, like hiring practices, can maintain the status quo, we fail to address a serious barrier to gender equality in the workplace.

Since certain hiring practices have been viewed as standard and used for so long, hiring managers and those in charge don't realize the massive misstep they are making. This creates a huge obstacle for women seeking positions in sales and sales leadership, because the system is not built to attract or include them.

A further obstacle encountered by women in the hiring process is **gender biased hiring**.

Gender biased hiring, as the name suggests, is the inclination or tendency to show preference to one candidate over another because of their gender. It is often not overt; it is unlikely that a hiring manager, when choosing between two candidates, will explicitly think, "We'll hire Richard instead of Emily, because Richard's a man and Emily is a woman!"

Instead, as you can probably guess, it tends to be more subtle. For example, research carried out by LinkedIn shows that when recruiters search for candidates, they tend to open men's LinkedIn profiles more often.[91] While active discrimination does exist, gender biased hiring is typically a bit more complicated and nuanced. As a result, it can almost be trickier to spot. So, how can gender biased hiring come about?

GENDER BIASED HIRING: A DEEP DIVE

It is reasonable to assume that often as part of the hiring process, the person responsible may have a certain idea of the kind of person who would be suited for the role or what kinds of traits they might have. This is true not only in sales, but across other industries. However, too often the association of certain traits with certain genders accompanies that assumption. Some roles may typically have people with supposedly feminine characteristics, which may prompt the hiring manager to unconsciously look for women.

What we have seen in sales is the assumption that the kind of person they are looking for is more masculine. For example, in more intense sales environments, they might look for hunters; someone who is confident, independent and a go-getter. Some may assume that these are traits more likely to be found in men, and so male candidates are the ones that are unconsciously drawn towards. Of course, this ignores the fact that many of the 'typical' traits that are perceived as being good for sales don't take into consideration the traits that makes one a good seller in the modern age, like empathy and active listening; traits that women usually possess.

The negative impacts of these preconceived notions and biases are multiplied when they are mixed with other kinds of bias, like similarity bias: the tendency to favor people who share character-istics or traits with us.

Unchecked similarity biases might mean that a hiring manager may be drawn to people who look more like them, or even if they went to the same university, or have similar contacts. While this can be a good basis to build up a rapport, it keeps the world of your organization small and insular. As touched on in the last chapter – having a diverse team is only beneficial!

However, in an environment where there is a majority of men, like in sales, there is a tendency to hire more men.

MARINA: *It's a harsh truth, but it's easier for white men to hire other white men because there's an inherent bias towards similarity. Women, on the other hand, are often naturally drawn to diversity. We* *understand the value of different perspectives, the richness that comes from a variety of backgrounds and experiences. We actively seek out and champion talent from underrepresented groups, broadening our pool of candidates and ultimately building stronger, more innovative teams.*

Companies with all male leadership teams can develop a reputation for being unwelcoming or unsupportive of diverse talent. This can negatively impact their employer brand and make it harder to attract top talent from all backgrounds. Seeing pictures on LinkedIn from company events that look like stag dos or bachelor parties, for example, is just disheartening because it paints a picture of a place with zero diversity.

If this mindset is common in the hiring process, we can assume it will crop up further down the line as well. When people only hire those like them, they will have a natural affinity towards those people as a working group. If this is the case, it's likely that they will continue to favor these 'like-minded' people in other aspects of their work life; there may be a greater understanding with their manager, and so a greater likelihood of promotion. When women are excluded from essential team-bonding and networking opportunities simply because they are female, their chances of being promoted can be negatively affected.

Ultimately, mixing with people outside of whom we relate to at work is something that we can all improve upon, and one that will only benefit us. If we broaden our network, we gain a wider understanding of what good can look like in a certain role. When it comes to hiring, that means that you can see the different kinds of traits that make someone thrive in their role, which then gives you a unique insight into the various applicants you encounter.

In essence, having a leadership team that is composed entirely of the same kind of person will create an echo chamber that reinforces existing biases, limits access to a wider talent pool, and ultimately hinders the company's ability to attract, retain, and develop the best and most diverse talent available. This limits the company's potential for innovation, growth, and market success.

You might already recognize the need to eradicate bias in the hiring process and make a more egalitarian environment, but you're thinking: Okay, that's great, but what can I do about it? Here are some active steps you can take to combat gender bias in the hiring process and ensure the future of your workplace is more diverse and equitable. We also consulted some of our external contributors, who shared their insights into crafting less biased hiring practices.

HOW TO COMBAT GENDER BIASED HIRING

Take a Closer Look at Job Descriptions

Research has shown that job descriptions can act as obstacles to women who want to enter sales and sales leadership positions, and that the wording of job descriptions can have a huge impact on the gender balance of applicants.

For example, a job listing might refer to the ideal candidate as 'he' – not necessarily because the person writing the listing envisions a man, but because they are using it as a default, in more of a gender neutral way. However, studies in a variety of languages continue to find that when job descriptions use 'he' in this way, it is still read overwhelmingly as male.[92] Furthermore, it has been found that women are also less likely to apply or perform well in interviews for jobs that are advertised using 'he' in a gender-neutral way.[93]

The different descriptors, too, can deter women from applying. A 2011 study by Danielle Gaucher and Justin Friesen discovered that using more 'masculine' words like "aggressive", "challenging", "decisive", or "competitive" in job descriptions lead to decreased interest in applying for female candidates.[94] This was not because the women thought they would not be able to do the job, but because they didn't think they would feel a sense of belonging in the workplace.[95] Similarly, when a European company put an emphasis on aggression and competitiveness in a job advertisement, alongside a stock photo of a man, only 5% of those who applied were women.[96]

To make job descriptions more attractive to female applicants, you should avoid typically 'masculine' language. The above study by Gaucher and Friesen found that using more 'feminine' words in job descriptions, like "interpersonal", "considerate", "honest", and "understanding", does not deter men at the same rate,[97] so if you change the wording of your job descriptions in this way, you do not run the risk of alienating male applicants. It's a win-win!

Part of this can be attributed to the fact that women tend to self-screen in job applications more often than men do; the LinkedIn study mentioned earlier found that women apply to 20% fewer jobs than men, and are 16% less likely than men to apply to a job after viewing it.[98]

What this means is that when you are looking for new talent, get advice and assistance from your peers or recruiters when crafting job descriptions to ensure they appeal to all potential applicants. When compiling the requirements for the role, ask yourself what really is a must-have and what is simply a nice-to-have. Instead of focusing on qualifications, center performance objectives; include not what they need to have already achieved, but rather what they will be expected to achieve in this role.

Other things to include in your job descriptions to appeal to female applicants is salaries. The previously mentioned LinkedIn study found that knowing the expected pay in a role is typically more important for women than it is for men.[99] It signals to the potential applicant that the organization prioritizes transparency and fair pay, no matter the candidate's gender or background.[100]

Coming up with job descriptions isn't easy – trying to suc-cinctly summarize your ideal candidate, and convince them to apply might seem like enough of a task even before you need to add more inclusive language. However, as we can tell from the research, when you put in the work, you will reap the rewards (a more diverse, awesome workforce!).

Here are some practical suggestions on creating job descriptions that will avoid some of these exclusionary pitfalls:

SUGGESTIONS ON CREATING INCLUSIVE JOB DESCRIPTIONS

1 Use Gender-Neutral Language.

- Use tools like Textio or Gender Decoder to identify and eliminate gender-coded words.

- Replace masculine-coded terms like "rockstar" or "ninja" with neutral terms like "expert" or "specialist."

- Focus on inclusive phrases such as "collaborative team player" instead of "strong leader."

2 Emphasize Growth and Flexibility

- Women are less likely than men to apply if they don't meet nearly all of the listed qualifications.

- Rephrase rigid requirements (e.g., "must have 10 years' experience") into flexible ones (e.g., "5+ years' experience preferred but not required").

- Highlight professional development opportunities and on-the-job training.

- Avoid listing an excessive number of "must-haves" and instead distinguish between "essential" and "preferred" qualifications.

3 Highlight Diversity and Inclusion Efforts

- Include a diversity statement in the job description, such as: "We are committed to building a diverse and inclusive team where everyone can thrive."
- Provide evidence of your DEI efforts, like gender representation stats or employee testimonials.
- Mention family-friendly benefits, such as flexible hours, parental leave, and remote work options.

Vary Your Hiring Team

To give potential female candidates and applicants a more equal opportunity, women need to be involved in the interview process. Studies have shown that women have a higher chance of being called back for jobs when the recruiter or hiring manager is female.[101] When you include women in the hiring process, you increase the chance of a connection between a female interviewee and interviewer, whatever form that may take. This can provide a female perspective on the candidate; there may be aspects or traits only they recognize. Furthermore, a female interviewer can make the female candidate feel more at ease, which will allow her to better convey her strengths. Not only that, having a woman on the hiring team communicates to prospective candidates that there is diversity in the company and that they will be entering into a welcoming environment. Differing points of view in your hiring team will also ensure you get the best person for the position, as they will have been vetted from several angles.

LUCY: *We have Cultural Ambassadors – a number of people from diverse groups who assist in the interview process. They're available to answer any questions a candidate may have, and ensure that the candidate can see first hand we have a diverse organization.*

However, it is important to note that if there are very few women in an organization who are senior enough to be involved in the hiring process, this could adversely affect them and their workload, which is another reason why we should strive for balanced leadership teams.

PENNY: *When I run interviews, I always make sure to have a panel who are different to me. Everyone has biases, and it can be hard to keep them in check when interviewing, but we try to hold each other accountable and to watch our leanings towards people like ourselves. It's also so important to not only have variety in gender in your hiring team, but in background and personality too, so candidates can see the different types of people and perspectives there are in your company. In addition, it brings rich and new perspectives where they may see qualities you have not picked up on.*

Stick to the System

If you set up a clear hiring process and stick to it, you can eliminate bias. For example, before resumes are reviewed by the hiring manager, ask HR or recruitment to remove the names and dates of birth from them. You should also ask them to remove pictures from the resumes.

These steps will remove even the potential for implicit biases to affect whether they are chosen. In the actual interview, make sure to have a set of questions laid out, along with a scorecard with evaluation criteria for each interviewee. Standardize the questions that you ask each candidate, and be thoughtful about how you phrase the questions so that they apply to all genders. For example, instead of asking them to describe themselves, ask how an old manager or peer would describe them.

By marking this criteria against a scoring system, it avoids bias and ensures candidates are judged for their skills and abilities, rather than based on a feeling. In tandem with this, you can use tasks or assessments to test for attributes and qualities that would align the candidate to the role and company culture.

As an example, when Gap is seeking to fill a vacancy, they set different assignments related to the role, and applicants who perform the best are sent to hiring managers without any identifying information. As a result, around 60% end up coming from underrepresented backgrounds.[102] By sticking to their process, the hiring managers avoid gender bias having an impact. To assess whether someone is fit for a role, you can include questions that align to core attributes, like coachability or resilience – the entire interview doesn't necessarily need to be about their experience.

ANNIE ANONYMOUS: *I went through a process recently, which was apparently consistent but it was not. I had more steps than my male counterparts, even though it was an internal move, and totally different interviewers. My team was not approached for feedback, yet the others' teams were. Consistency in process is so important to have fair and understood outcomes.*

Reconsider the Shortlist

Expanding the pool that you hire from will not only give you access to a number of qualified individuals who you may have previously overlooked, it will also help you remove gender bias in the hiring process.

When working with recruiters, for example, ensure that they provide an even number of candidates who have diverse education backgrounds and genders. You can outline that you aren't just looking for experience, but specific attributes, like being coachable, resilient, or driven. As a result, you will have a better likelihood of hiring more diverse candidates.

When hiring for leadership positions, it is likely that those recruiting will have an informal shortlist of potential candidates in mind, particularly if they're recruiting internally. Believe it or not, but spending a little extra time compiling that list, informal or otherwise, can have an impact on counteracting gender biased hiring. As can happen, even before posting the job ad, it's possible that there are already potential candidates who will be favored over others. Maybe someone they know from another organization who they know is eager to change roles, or a skilled former colleague, or someone they met at a networking event. But the odds are that this will negatively affect the female candidates.

In industries like sales, where men tend to make up a high percentage of the workforce, people often automatically think, as we have mentioned previously, that men are therefore more suited for those roles. And so, a hiring manager's informal pre-existing shortlist is more likely to consist of more men than women, if not only men. A study carried out by the Harvard Business Review found that when you extend your initial shortlist of potential candidates, the number of women included increases by 33%.[103] Since it asks the person hiring to spend more time thinking, they will be less likely to go with their immediate thoughts and consider those who may not have come to mind at first, but who could still be perfect for the role.

By adding a few more candidates to your shortlist, even if it's an informal one, you can increase its gender diversity and reduce the odds that you will leave out a qualified female candidate simply because male candidates came to mind at first.

In addition to this, you can broaden your hiring pool by working alongside HR to improve benefits that attract a wider range of people. We discussed the importance of job flexibility for many women, for example. Remember that people are attracted to a role not just for the job, but everything surrounding it.

Hiring is an essential step to increase the amount of women in sales and sales leadership. You can't have more female sales leaders if you don't have any female salespeople, and you won't get any female salespeople if you don't give them a fair chance at the recruitment stage. By following the advice we have outlined, you can implement more egalitarian hiring practices that can boost not only the amount of female applicants you see, but also the amount of successful female candidates. To surmount gender-biased hiring, the answer isn't just to ignore it.

Someone who is misguided might say, "We want to hire more women, but we just aren't getting any applicants who have what we're looking for!" As we have covered, it isn't that simple. It takes a conscious effort.

If you communicate to potential candidates how committed your organization is to diversity and equality, and yours is an environment in which they will thrive, you will attract and interview the best candidates, regardless of gender or background.

Of course, once you do hire more women, you need to make sure you retain them. Fostering that supportive environment will nourish female sellers, as well as attracting more to your organization – but more on that in the next chapter.

Chapter 10: Hiring

- Take a closer look at your job descriptions to make their wording more inclusive.

- When you receive resumes, work with HR to remove gender and age identifiers to eliminate biases.

- Vary your hiring and interview team for mixed perspectives.

- Have a specific interview process that you stick to and metrics that you evaluate candidates by.

- Broaden your net – don't just look for the typical candidates you expect to hire.

Chapter Eleven

ALLYSHIP

To create a sales environment that is welcoming to all, we need as many people as possible advocating for it. People in the minority can speak up all they want, but their voices don't always carry as far as the majority's. Allyship challenges and disrupts unconscious and conscious bias to instead foster a culture that is inclusive and recognizes performance based on merit. Visible support from both male and female allies signals to women that they belong. Allyship provides emotional support that reduces imposter syndrome and helps them feel valued and engaged, and increases performance.

In a male-dominated industry like tech sales, men who champion and act as allies for their female colleagues play a pivotal role not only in the success of the individual, but in the success of the organization as a whole.

Allyship underpins a large part of creating an inclusive environment. Here we are focusing on how you as a peer and manager can support and elevate your female colleagues. It includes listening to your female colleagues and being mindful of situations in which they might be sidelined.

It means intervening if you encounter sexist or poor behaviors to set an example and change something that was normalized and accepted for so long. It means educating yourself on issues that might not affect you, but affect those around you. When someone is an active ally, the impact can be huge.

With organizations embracing formal DEI programs and training, things are slowly changing and there is more education out there. But despite this knowledge, there still seems to be a hesitation to truly embrace allyship in the workplace.

But why?

A study conducted by Catalyst found that 74% of men named fear as a barrier to their being allies.[104] Fear of what, you might wonder? The study found that it can be attributed to three pathways, some of which are unconscious:

1. Fear of making mistakes and being criticized for trying to take action intended to reduce gender bias
2. Fear of negative judgements from other men
3. Fear of losing status if women were to achieve equality.

Let's take a closer look at these fears.

The fear of making mistakes and being criticized is fair; it comes from a place of wanting to do good but not being sure of the best way to do so. Research has shown that approximately 84% of men want to interrupt sexist behaviors in the workplace, but only 36% of men feel confident doing so.[105] They may want to help, but are worried about saying or doing the wrong thing. Nor do they want to make things worse by saying something when their female colleague would rather they didn't.

The fear of negative judgment from others is understandable. In a male-dominated space, it makes sense that your first instinct is to be more like those around you. However, the men who would judge you for vocally being an ally for your female colleagues are

the ones who most need to hear it! We will return to the importance of this later, but the best way to counteract bad behavior is to
challenge it. As a leader there are ways that you can create an environment where your team has trust among them to speak freely
and challenge each other; when you create that environment where
colleagues speak up not just for women but for all members. When
you create an environment that is actively supportive of women,
you communicate to everyone what is and isn't acceptable, and that
is how you make real change.

In a competitive world, the initial flinch that is the fear of losing
status makes sense. Interestingly, in her book, "Alpha Male and
Alpha Female: Top International Managers on Gender Diversity
and Mixed Leadership", Bettina Al-Sadik-Lowinski interviewed
28 male management board members from 11 countries on the
topic of diversity.[106] Al-Sadik-Lowinski found, among other
things, that some male CEOs are not comfortable with having
women at leadership level.[107] The interviews conducted showed
that men on management boards often have a strong fear of public
embarrassment by female colleagues. They tend to criticize women
they perceive as overly assertive, and when they are challenged by
such women, they may react with hostility, says Al-Sadik-Lowinski.[108]

There is of course no need for this. Making room for more
women at the top in sales organizations doesn't necessarily mean
that those already there will lose status. Status that can be lost
simply because of more egalitarian hiring practices and allyship
is probably not something attained by real achievement anyway.
If we instead focus on what is to be gained by a more balanced
workplace – fresh perspectives, a rejuvenated talent pool – we
create a more meritocratic space for all.

WHY IS BEING AN ALLY IMPORTANT?

1. Studies have shown that diversity in teams and leadership leads to improved revenue growth and innovation. When people act as allies, they create a supportive environment that helps underrepresented talent thrive and boosts the ecosystem of the whole organization.
2. The inclusivity that comes with allyship builds trust and a great culture in your team and organization. This will increase retention, growth, and productivity, and when trying to grow a diverse culture, you will be more likely to retain top talent, including your female talent.
3. The organizational culture and thriving workforce that will come from intentional allyship will set your company as a great role model for all coming after, establishing standards to reach for.

So what do you do if you're a man and you want to act as an ally, but you don't know where to begin?

HOW DO YOU BECOME THE BEST ALLY YOU CAN BE?

Dive into Learning

A study by Gartner found that 86% of male sales leaders say women have the same opportunities for advancement as men, but only 61% of women say the same.[109] If a problem doesn't directly affect you, it makes sense why you might not notice how widespread it is. This is why education is such an important part of allyship – it shows you why you are putting your hat in the ring to support those around you.

Studies have shown that if you believe that you are totally

objective and not at all biased, you are actually more likely to let biases influence your behavior and how you treat those around you.[110] But if you don't take into consideration that everyone has biases that may negatively affect those around them, you can't take measures to lessen their impact. No one wants to think that they are biased in any way. Understandably, the idea makes us uncomfortable. But embracing that discomfort is actually the key to progress. When you identify the problem, you can start to solve it.

Educating yourself on how women might be negatively affected in the workplace and the behaviors that lead to that is an essential element of creating a more egalitarian workplace, and lays the groundwork for true empathy for you as a leader. This education can take any form; there are countless articles, books, and podcasts that dive into challenges women and minorities encounter in the workplace in general and sales specifically.

SOME OF OUR RECOMMENDATIONS

BOOKS	PODCASTS	TED TALKS
Invisible Women - Caroline Criado Perez	**The Broad Experience** **The Guilty Feminist**	*How to be a great ally -* Melina Epler
Lean In - Sheryl Sandberg		*We should all be feminists -* Chimamanda Ngozi Adichie
How Women Rise - Sally Helgesen and Marshall Goldsmith		
How to Make it Happen: Turning Failure into Success - Maria Hatzistefanis		
The Let Them Theory - Mel Robbins		

Be Proactive

We saw previously that a high percentage of men want to be allies to their female colleagues, but not as many feel they know how best to do it. This is understandable, but a fundamental part of being an ally is being proactive in doing so. Part of that means being open to listening to your colleagues and learning from them and being open to understanding the concerns of marginalized groups and what they go through, without judgment. There are some easy ways to do this.

1. Take time to speak to your female team members, and get to know them. Ask for their input on how they are feeling in the team, and whether there are any areas for improvement. You can also ask other leaders in the industry who are known to have diverse teams that champion women – what is their advice?

2. Lead by example and speak up in a healthy way for inclusivity. Don't be afraid to be the lone voice in the room.

3. Be mindful of the words that you use. If words are not used correctly, they can be misinterpreted.

4. Be prepared to stand up and take action when you see micro-aggressions and other negative behavior. When it comes to people who contribute (knowingly or unknowingly) to a negative environment, sometimes they will only listen to feedback from those like them. While women can certainly stand up for themselves, in a male-dominated industry like tech sales, they might not feel comfortable doing so, or may not even be in the room to defend themselves.

5. Amplify women's voices. By ensuring their ideas are acknowledged in group discussions, you create a better overall balance in the team, and contribute to a more equitable environment.

To make meaningful change for gender equality, it's important for men to be involved in discussions on diversity and inclusion. Look into diversity initiatives that you can be an active participant in, or offer mentorship to your female colleagues or team members who you think would benefit.

In the interest of supporting our colleagues, it can seem better to wait for their cue to step up and do so, but being proactive and putting in effort to learn from and support the women in your organization can create a better environment for everyone.

PENNY: *Allyship takes many forms. One of my managers led by example, setting clear expectations for meetings: ensure every voice is heard, do not interrupt, and always show respect. And he didn't just say it – he enforced it. Over time, these principles were just part of the team DNA, and I always felt heard and supported.*

ANNIE ANONYMOUS: *I couldn't count the number of times I've been called 'babe', 'hun', 'darling', or 'sweetheart' by people at work. It's so disrespectful. I also get really frustrated when people refer to me as 'she' rather than by name in a meeting.*

MARINA: *Leadership isn't just about setting strategy; it's about setting standards. When we witness disrespectful behavior, we have a responsibility to address it immediately, sending a clear message about what's acceptable and what's not. In a QBR, just as in any meeting, attention is a form of respect. I've often seen people returning to their phone after presenting, which sends a message of disengagement and undermines the collective effort – I would always call this out in the moment in the room.*

RICH PEREZ, RVP AT GRAFANA LABS, ON ADVICE FOR HIS YOUNGER SELF:

Go sit in a room full of female sales professionals and see how it feels, because that is how they feel everyday. In that room, I'm a minority, I stand out. I have to be careful of what I'm going to say, and I'm nervous!

AS SAID BY RONAL KARIA, VP OF SALES (CENTRAL AND NORTHERN EUROPE) AT SLACK:

Something I've seen people struggle with is that casual sexism, when others make comments are jokes without even thinking about it. They might seem like little things, but they're not little, and it's so important to call those things out. Even in your friend groups! I've actually called out friends of mine, saying things like "You can't say that, it's not appropriate." If no one calls it out, it's almost accepted by the silence, and that's not okay.

PENNY: *Some ways to foster inclusivity are; Encourage everyone to actively listen and include diverse perspectives in each discussion, ensuring all voices are genuinely heard and valued. Make inclusivity a shared responsibility by setting clear DEI goals and regularly acknowledging inclusive behaviors across the team, and provide fair access to development and mentoring opportunities, supporting every team member's growth based on their unique strengths and contributions. The ultimate goal is for everyone to hold each other to account and for people to feel comfortable doing it with each other, not just me as the manager calling it out.*

<u>Lead by Example</u>

Once you stand up for and support the women around you, you inspire others to do the same. When you champion them and get involved in events and panels, you set a standard that people can look to and reach for.

When there is a precedent set at the top for allyship, be that in the form of speaking up or making a point to hire talented female sales leaders, other men are less likely to fear repercussions if they do the same, and will know that any of the negative behaviors we have highlighted will not be tolerated.

What you do influences those around you, especially when you are in a leadership position. Openly advocating for the women in your team and organization demonstrates the degree to which you should support those around you, particularly those who may be in the minority.

Another crucial element is recognizing and celebrating achievements if you want to foster a positive environment and motivate individuals. The most effective way to increase awareness is by publicly highlighting these accomplishments, showcasing the contributions and successes of team members to inspire others.

HOW DO YOU BECOME THE BEST ALLY YOU CAN BE?

Dive into learning and educate yourself about struggles faced by women in sales, as well as unconscious biases you could have that may be holding you back

Be proactive and make an effort to champion the women around you and learn from them

Call out negative behavior and demonstrate what is and isn't acceptable

Lead by example and encourage other men to become allies too

Push your team to engage with large groups of people

HOW DOES BEING AN ALLY MAKE A DIFFERENCE?

In sales leadership, there are still some rooms that women aren't as present in. When the people in those rooms speak up on their behalf, it means that women aren't advocating for things alone. There's strength in numbers.

Acting as allies not only creates an environment that is more inclusive to all, it creates one that makes it clear that negative or exclusionary behaviors are not tolerated. The culture that comes as a result will have a real and positive impact on the entire organization.

Allyship isn't just something you can do as an individual, but something you can spread team-wide. Leaders who are allies can build a wider environment where they are pioneers of inclusivity and where women can thrive. This change can happen as a leader of a team but also at a company-wide level within policies and training programs. Not only that, they can model the behavior they expect from their teams.

The inclusive behavior this inspires means team members are wholeheartedly there for each other, which will cause the sense of trust in the team to increase exponentially.

Ultimately, this trust is the cornerstone of all performance and business. Without trust, your team is not going to feel comfortable taking risks, because they will not feel safe to fail. Taking risks is the only way to grow, and so trust is essential.

Trust strengthens, and is strengthened by, psychological safety, which occurs when team members share the belief that they can take risks, voice ideas and concerns, ask questions, and acknowledge mistakes without fear of negative repercussions.[111] Psychological safety leads to better motivation and decision making and helps foster a culture of continuous improvement. Studies have found that who is on a team matters less than how that team works together, and so psychological safety is a must for high-performing teams.[112] Allyship plays a huge role in this.

Allies can step in for their female colleagues who might not feel comfortable speaking out, and they can set a standard for how everyone is to be treated (with respect!). By educating themselves on the issues that might not explicitly affect them, allies can gain further insights into what they can do to further champion the women around them. When allies are in leadership positions, they hold the power to support their female team members and remove obstacles that may be in their way.

In sales, if you're hardworking and persistent, you can achieve a lot. So, if everyone in an organization promotes and pushes for an egalitarian culture where everyone can thrive, it will succeed. That is where allyship is instrumental.

Chapter 11: Allyship

Male allies play a crucial role in fostering an inclusive environment in tech sales by supporting and advocating for their female colleagues. A culture of allyship leads to stronger teams, increased trust, higher retention rates, and improved business performance.

Being an ally requires action, not just intention. This includes listening to female colleagues, amplifying their voices, challenging biases, and intervening when witnessing microaggressions. Leading by example and fostering an inclusive environment are essential steps in driving real change.

When men in leadership positions openly advocate for women, participate in diversity initiatives, and highlight achievements, they set a precedent that normalizes allyship and discourages negative behaviors.

Chapter Twelve

MATERNITY MATTERS

In the last year that we've been working on this book, we have been fortunate enough to talk to a number of women at different stages in their sales journeys.

Throughout these conversations, recurring themes that kept cropping up were anxieties or stresses about starting a family or generally being a mother while working in sales. Some of these worries included:

- A negative impact on them getting a promotion or key account allocations if it was known they were planning on having a family
- Loss of key accounts or coverage while away on maternity leave
- Loss of earnings on any owed commission or pay rises as a result of being on maternity leave
- A lack of flexibility when they come back to work
- The terms of the maternity policy and protection

When looking at the career trajectory of women in software sales, we end up seeing the numbers of women at different levels decrease as you look further up the ladder. We previously mentioned the 2023 McKinsey Women in the Workplace study which painted this picture perfectly.

| PERCENTAGE OF WOMEN IN SOFTWARE IN 2023

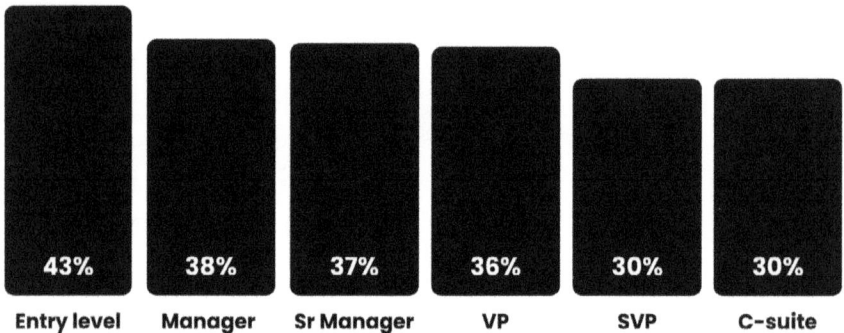

Entry level	Manager	Sr Manager	VP	SVP	C-suite
43%	38%	37%	36%	30%	30%

With that, there is a huge drop off of women at and around the age of 35 which would usually be when we see people coming into the role of VP or SVP. We believe that some of this is impacted by women not coming back to work – or moving into other roles – post maternity

In this section, we intend to highlight the real challenges that women face today in coming back to work, or staying in sales, getting into management and remaining until Exec level and to showcase examples of what individual contributors, leaders and organizations are doing to improve this.

To do this, we have included real life stories from both men and women with three points of view:

1. Women who have gone on maternity leave and come back, delving into what has worked well, what hasn't, and how they have been successful
2. Female and male sales leaders with tips on the steps they have taken to make changes in their teams
3. Innovative policies and approaches organizations have in place.

WHAT DOES THE DATA SAY?

To effectively encourage women to come back to sales once they've had a baby, we first need to understand the reasons for their departure. At a general level, women tend to exit full-time employment and even the labor market after having children at a higher rate than men; a 2019 study by the UK Government Equalities Office found that three years after having a baby, 37% of mothers were in full-time employment in comparison to 61% of fathers, and 33% of mothers were unemployed, in comparison to just over 10% of fathers.[113]

Poor maternity leave policies can be a factor to women withdrawing from certain positions. Numerous studies worldwide have found that having a good maternity leave has a positive impact on keeping women in the workforce.[114] Not enough time off following childbirth could result in an organization losing women who had just given birth at twice the rate of other employees, as happened at Google until they extended maternity leave from three months with partial pay to five months with full pay, which caused the attrition rate to drop 50%.[115]

As we have seen, across corporations, the percentage of women present in leadership positions decreases significantly the further up the ladder you go. A 2024 Gartner report found that only 30% of senior sales leaders are women.[116] At least part of this can be attributed to the so-called 'motherhood penalty', which manifests itself in perceptions of lower competence and commitment, higher professional expectations, fewer opportunities for hiring and promotion, and lower salary recommendations.[117] A 2007 study found that mothers were seen as 12.1 percentage points less committed to their jobs compared to non-mothers.[118]

JACQUELINE DE GERNIER, SVP AND HEAD OF GLOBAL NEW BUSINESS AT GWI:

"I did an INSEAD course on leading gender diversity programs, and I learned about what they call the 'mummy track': when people make assumptions when women go back to work that they won't want to do the long hours, that they won't be prepared to put the customer first, and that they won't be able to do what the role requires. Rather than saying to the person, "What would you like and how can you continue to be successful with your career goals?" they make assumptions in closed rooms. Then they get passed over for promotion and leadership roles, or they get suggested for customer success roles rather than sales roles.

If organizations want a more balanced workforce, they need to put measures in place to support both their employees who are considering having children and those who already do. To increase the amount of women in senior leadership positions, there needs to be incentives in place for women to return to work after having children.

For individuals who want to or are thinking about going on maternity leave, it is important to be as informed as possible, so you know what you can expect, and also to know what to ask for as you put a plan in place."

DOES HAVING CHILDREN IMPACT A WOMAN'S CAREER IN SALES?

One of the significant things noted by nearly all the parents working in sales is that when you have a baby, your priorities may shift, but by no means should this negatively impact your career.

For example, when we spoke to Flavia Brown, then Regional

Director at Multiverse, she was in her fourth month of maternity leave, intending to go back to work after six months. Part of this, she said, was because she thought she may miss out on a promotion. "Not because of any discrimination, but just because if you're not in a role and the business has a need for that immediate need for that position, one can't fulfill that need if you are on extended leave." However, she was promoted to her new role as Area Vice President before she returned to work.

Upon returning, she told us that still, if you want to have children, particularly as a mother, "You have to accept that your career is likely to change; your career may slow down and you may want it to. Before you go on maternity leave, you will think that's the worst possible thing, but after you have had a baby your priorities do change. I was nervous about going back to work, but now having come back to work, I am loving it. I feel so lucky to return in a new and more senior role, as it's helped to give me a lot of perspective to what is most important in life, whilst making me better at my job, in terms of prioritization and managing my energy to give more value to the team."

While having children may change the way you work, it doesn't need to impact your career. That being said, it's not always easy. It takes a combination of hard work and organizing from the woman as well as support from family, partner and organization.

HOW HAVE WOMEN NAVIGATED THE TRANSITION BACK TO WORK?

This is true in any industry, but particularly in sales: women can be a mum and have rewarding careers where they are high achievers and, but the success of that transition back to work after maternity leave is largely dependent on the support they receive.

PENNY: *You absolutely can be successful and be a mother but* *it really does depend on the support you have at home and in the workplace. I was fortunate to remain top performer across both times I had my two children, but it would have been harder without the support of my husband and mum. That being said, I found that being in sales gave me flexibility with the hours I worked. There were times when I would need to come home to put the kids to bed but would log on after they went to bed. My manager trusted me as I hit my targets and worked hard.*

Many women we spoke to talked about how essential having a supportive partner and network is to their ability to be successful in sales. Navigating childcare is a crucial part of modern parenthood, particularly in sales, when meetings may be at unconventional times or travel might be necessary. For Kate Hunt, Regional Director at Salesforce, that meant needing to hire a nanny for three days a week, who she can't live without. The main reason for hiring the nanny, Kate said, was because, "Before that point, my husband and I would get into these Top Trumps conversations about who had the more important meeting. It was like, 'I've got an MD on this call,' 'Well, I've got a CEO.' For a true co-parenting thing, there's always a winner and always a perceived loser. Someone has to do the pickup while the other person takes the call. And to be honest, that puts humongous pressure on our marriage. It's daily stress to try and rota it. So then we had to also get a nanny, and I threw myself into work to be able to afford that."

For some, hiring a nanny is a necessity because they cannot rely on family to help with childcare – several of the women we spoke to mentioned the assumption that family would help look after children, something which is unrealistic if you don't have close family nearby. Conversely, others need to rely on family when they cannot afford a nanny.

Undoubtedly, having people you can turn to for childcare and general household tasks, as well as general emotional support, is essential to navigate the transition back to work. But what happens when there isn't that support at work?

Kate Hunt told us about having a serious burnout that might have been prevented if someone at her workplace had encouraged her to slow down.

"I hit the wall at a million miles an hour, and I didn't realize how bad it was until I lost my memory, and I lost my words. I came home one day and I was talking to my husband, and I just couldn't get my words out correctly.

I meant to say to him 'I'm going to bed, I don't feel well,' but what I actually said was, 'I'm going out in the car.'

Later, he mentioned his sister, and I said, "I don't know her." He showed me photos, but there was no recognition. He had to call 999; I had a stress-induced migraine, which had never happened to me before. I had just caused so much stress and anxiety that it caused this stress induced migraine that caused me to lose my memory for about four hours.

And I think part of why that happened was because no one called me out on my behaviors. When you're seen as highly successful, you're just left alone to do your thing, which means no one's stopping you, no one is checking in.

Because I was deeply motivated to succeed, I was trying to do my job to the best of my ability and then come home and be this magical mum, who does bathtime, bedtime and everything. I can't say no to anything. But no one around me said, 'Sit down.' Don't get me wrong, my manager was amazing, but I think on reflection, I probably wasn't honest about how much I was pushing myself and working. So, it was the killer combination of wanting to impress at work as well as not wanting to drop the ball at home and with my kids. I think if someone had recognized what was happening and pointed it out in terms of my behavior at work, like sending emails at unhealthy hours, it might have made a difference."

Kate also pointed out that she has completely learned from this story and adjusted her life to make sure it doesn't happen again. "I'm still successful in my job, but not putting myself in the hospital anymore!"

A supportive manager and team plays a pivotal role in successfully transitioning back to work after having a child; having the people around you be there for you had a massive impact for nearly every woman we spoke to.

Thea Petch, Client Director at Snowflake told us, "When I found out I was pregnant, I cried in the toilet at work because I didn't know what it would mean for my career. I called a senior leader in my team to tell her and she said, 'I'm not going to let you fail.' And she didn't. My team built a project around me going on maternity; I had two global accounts and some major accounts, and I was worried I would lose them. My team, even though they had their own responsibilities that were very important, they offered to take my accounts and look after them for me, and they didn't want to take any of my commission."

The lack of support from managers can push mothers away from organizations. Jacqueline de Gernier told us about how she felt when her boss was unsympathetic about her frequently needing to leave work to look after her son when he got sick at nursery.

"I'm sure it's the same with every child, but when my son first went to nursery he just picked up every bug that was going around, so my husband or I would need to drop things to race home and pick him up because he was running a temperature or whatever it was. I had a new boss at the time, and I remember getting a lot of questions from him. The final straw for me was at one point, he took me out for coffee and told me all about the childcare arrangements that he and his wife had and how well that worked for him. But we couldn't afford a nanny!

I just thought, 'How dare you?' In those early years, you're hanging on by a thread anyway, and we were really pedaling hard to do our best.

So in the end, that was why I moved from that company. When I left, I told the CEO, one of the founders, why, and he was mortified. He said, 'I had no idea any of this was going on. Why didn't you tell us?' He was so upset." Being in a place where you can trust your manager and your team to have your back when you go on maternity leave and come back is imperative to mastering that transition.

FLEXIBILITY

Something else that stood out as essential to the successful transition back to work after maternity leave is flexibility.

PENNY: *One of the benefits of being in sales is the flexibility it can offer. This doesn't necessarily mean less hours, but rather smart working and focus on impact. The job is so performance related it's easy to see success or not. In my teams I am less worried about the hours they work, but more the type of work they are doing. We are all humans who have a family and life outside of work, so I make sure I don't put team meetings at school/nursery pick up or drop off times where I can, and respect the importance of balancing home and work life.*

For many women, the difference between staying in a role or leaving it can come down to flexible work policies. 15% of women listed lack of flexibility around working hours as a reason they left their jobs.[119] Furthermore, 21% of women who wanted to leave their jobs listed lack of flexibility as a reason.[120] Even when roles are not able to offer that flexibility, it is important to recognize the impact the lack of flexibility could have.

LYNDSEY REES POWLES, AVP DIGITAL SALES AT SPLUNK, ON LACK OF FLEXIBILITY:

Returning from maternity leave after nine months with my son was a bittersweet experience. The excitement of rejoining the company and team I loved was overshadowed by the anxiety of balancing my new role as a mother with professional responsibilities. I had settled into a four-day workweek, having a nanny three days a week and family help one day a week which felt like a perfect compromise, allowing me to devote quality time to my son while also contributing to my career. However, when my new manager presented me with an ultimatum to switch to a five-day week contract, this made me upset and angry as there was no consideration or empathy for my transition and agreed contract. I was torn between my passion for my job and my dedication to my family, leaving me frustrated and overwhelmed. I decided to leave the company as his actions made me resent him and I thought the relationship would be untenable. I wanted to work for someone that respected me and my transition back to work.

In the modern work landscape, flexible working has become much more commonplace; days working from home, for example, are something that everyone in a team can benefit from, but which can make the life of a woman returning to work after maternity leave much easier. When we spoke to Flavia Brown, she told us that she had so much respect for women working high power jobs while being mums before COVID made flexible working more common, because she had no idea how they did it. She said, "I'm going back to work after six months maternity leave soon, and I'm just so glad that I can work from home two or three days a week. That's not a new flexibility policy for me, it's company wide. Parents need that flexibility, because most schools finish at three – and women still have societal pressure to be the one who handles the social calendar, or manages the childcare."

In order to make flexibility in a role work, returning mothers often learn to be more efficient with their time.

AS SAID BY JACQUELINE DE GERNIER:

> *I became so much more efficient and so much more productive in my time when I became a mum. You are totally focused on the outcomes as opposed to just being busy. When I went on maternity leave before having my son, I had negotiated that when I returned I would do a four day work week but carry the full quota. That took a lot of negotiation, but I basically sold it to them like this: I think I can do in four days what everyone else is doing in five, and frankly what I used to do in five. I was absolutely successful in that, and I managed to carry that policy forward into the next two companies.*

For women returning after maternity leave, being given the space to be flexible with how they work while remaining committed to delivering (and often over-delivering) can be the difference between succeeding in a role and leaving it.

WHAT STEPS HAVE LEADERS TAKEN TO HELP WOMEN SUCCESSFULLY COME BACK TO WORK IN SALES?

For women to successfully return to work after maternity leave, leaders need to have their backs. But what does that look like? We spoke to a number of leaders to get their insights on what can be done to make a sales work environment that is welcoming for returning mothers.

Focus on Results

As we touched on above, focusing on output and results rather than the appearance of being present is a key element. For Stephanie McLaurin, Head of Sales at Birdie, it's an essential part of supporting not just those of her team who are parents, but everyone. "Someone shouldn't feel stressed that they have to do one thing over the other," she said. "So if someone needs to leave early to pick up their child, or look after their child instead of working, I just try to completely support them and take that pressure off their shoulders."

Lead by Example

Part of leadership is modeling behavior you hope your team will replicate. This can take a lot of forms, but to make a comfortable environment for mothers returning to work there are two main aspects people we spoke to pointed out:

1. Setting boundaries
2. Being open and vulnerable

Setting boundaries as a leader not only gives you more space for your personal life, it sets a standard for your team. As Mark Dando, GM EMEA North at SUSE, said, "I make time for the school run every Wednesday, and I will never compromise on school plays and events like parents' evenings; I'm publicly very vocal about saying, 'I can't make this because I'm going to do something with the kids.'"

When a leader is vulnerable with their team, it opens the door for the team to be vulnerable as well. When you create the space for the team to share what they're struggling with, be it childcare/ parenting related or not, it removes the stress that may come with feeling like there is something to hide.

Ramp Time

Something sales leaders can do is introduce a ramp-up time following maternity leave. Amending quotas to allow for returning mothers to adjust and get back into the swing of things can help them feel less overwhelmed about the return to work. If there is resistance to these policies, it is important to remember the cost comparison between ramping up someone returning from maternity leave versus a new hire. While the former may need some time to get back to where they were, they are already familiar with the way your business is run, and how the job is done, while the latter will need to be entirely acclimated to your organization.

FROM OLLIE SHARPE, CRO AT TRUMPET:

There is a ridiculous range of what different SaaS companies do in paying maternity for people. Some companies pay something like OTE (on-target earnings) for X amount of time, for quite a long time, and then you have other companies that are purely paying basic salary or paying it only for a very short period of time. A salesperson gets used to earning what they earn, so when a woman takes time off to have a baby but they don't earn as much as they're used to (I saw one that was 75% of OTE, no matter how much they'd been earning), you're putting pressure on them to come back before they're ready.

Coverage of Accounts

An issue that arises for salespeople going on maternity leave and for their leaders is what to do with their accounts. Do they all get reassigned, and so when they return they have to start from scratch? When we spoke to Mark Dando, he explained that they have a process in place known as 'guesting', which is used for anyone who is going to own an account for less than a year (people leaving, new starters) and works well with maternity leave.

A guesting rep is responsible for managing the accounts, but not for achieving a quota tied to those accounts. However, they still receive commission on any deals closed during that time, and quota relief, which means the deals will still count towards reducing their overall sales targets.

"The payoff," he told us, "is that you generate pipeline. If you can't close that pipeline, then you need to hand that over. When someone returns to work, there's a three month handover period; month one, you'll get 100%, month two, you'll get 50%. That then drives an earlier closure. For the person who owns the account, it's still being actively managed, and they won't lose out on pipeline."

WHAT STEPS HAVE ORGANIZATIONS TAKEN TO HELP WOMEN SUCCESSFULLY COME BACK TO WORK IN SALES?

We don't pretend to have all the answers. What organizations do to support women returning to work from maternity leave is largely dependent on what each organization is capable of and the willingness of individuals to advocate for certain changes. To give an idea of what is achievable and has been successful elsewhere, we spoke to a number of people across our industry to help prospective mothers and those advocating for better workplace policies ideas of where to start.

Maternity Policy

As we've touched on, lack of good maternity compensation can have a serious negative impact on women in technology sales. It is a payment inequality that can contribute to your organization's overall gender pay gap; in the US, the pay gap between mothers and married fathers is three times higher than the pay gap between men and women without children.[121] What we have seen when it comes to maternity policies varies hugely; sometimes depending on the size of the organization, sometimes depending on how dedicated they are to retaining their returning mothers.

When Flavia Brown went on maternity leave, she worked with her leadership to make a case for a different maternity policy when it came to sales. "The overall package is now different from other departments, as it should be, because salespeople get paid differently due to commission. We came to an agreement that saw me getting paid commission for team performance when I was out, due to the work and investment in the deals before I left."

For Kate Hunt, at Salesforce, they took the average of her on-target earnings (OTE) and paid her accordingly during her leave. For salespeople who go on leave, it's important for organizations to take into account that a large percentage of their pay usually comes from commission.

When organizations don't properly compensate their salespeople on maternity leave, they put pressure on them to come back sooner than they are ready. It sets a poor example for other people who want to go on maternity leave in the future.

PENNY: *Seventeen years ago, when I had my first child, things* *were very different. I was the first woman at my American company to go on maternity leave – there wasn't even a policy in place. My boss's immediate reaction was, 'Okay, who can I give your accounts to so the business isn't impacted?' I worked closely with HR to create a fair maternity policy, including commission payments. It was a battle, and not something I should have had to go through, but we came to a fair agreement in the end. More importantly, it set the foundation for a proper policy that supported the women who came after me.*

Paternity Leave

Something that came up both in our research for this book and the conversations around it was the necessity not just for better maternity policies, but for better paternity policies. Not only does the data indicate that when paternity leave is paid properly paternity leave, there is a positive impact on female employment,[122] having a partner there to support a new mother can have a huge impact. For Stephanie MacLaurin, her husband taking paternity leave was monumental, both immediately after the birth of her child and when she was returning to work.

"My husband had sixteen weeks of paternity leave, which was really amazing," she told us. "I had a C-section, so having my husband with me for six weeks as I had to recover from the birth was so important. He was my absolute rock. What it also meant was that when I was returning to work, he was able to take more paternity leave, and he was responsible for transitioning our child into full-time nursery. That meant that when I was going back to work, I wasn't trying to juggle a child starting nursery and then also keep my life together; he was able to take on that responsibility so I could focus my efforts and my attention on my work."

Ultimately, there is a lot to be achieved in terms of setting women up for success when they go and return from maternity leave in sales. A lot of the discussions and focus on parental leave tend to presume a 'typical' two parent, heterosexual household. Women we spoke to in same-sex relationships expressed the need for greater awareness of non-conventional family structures in order for a more comfortable and welcoming workplace environment.

Hannah Ajikawo, CEO and founder at Revenue Funnel, told us about the reactions she received at work when pregnant while in a gay relationship. "I'll never forget these two things that happened when I told people I was pregnant. The first, men, always men, would come up to me and ask, 'So, how did you have a baby? What did you do?' As if it was a normal conversation – and these were grown men who were about ten years older than me. That was very awkward, and I felt obligated to respond.

The second, this woman had come back from leave, and she didn't know I was nearby but I overheard her saying, 'I didn't even know she liked men.' I was just shocked. It was just an outright disrespectful environment, and I was just thinking, 'Why would that come out of your mouth?'"

We are on the cusp of a cultural shift when it comes to work-life balance and a better environment for everyone wanting to go on parental leave – but it is the responsibility of individuals and organizations to drive this change forward.

We hope that this section has provided both individuals looking to start families and thrive in sales and those who manage them with tangible tips and insights into how they can navigate this transition and come back stronger. As a result, we will see more balanced leadership teams, C-suites and board rooms, which will only serve to benefit our organizations and industry.

Chapter 12: Maternity Matters

Women's successful return to work after maternity leave in sales depends on a combination of personal effort, support from family and partners, and flexibility from the workplace, such as adjusted work hours or working from home.

Supportive managers and teams that adjust workloads or offer ramp-up time are crucial for women returning from maternity leave. A lack of empathy from leadership can drive employees away, as seen in cases where unsympathetic attitudes toward family responsibilities led to departures.

Maternity policies should account for commission-based pay in sales roles, ensuring financial support during leave. Equally, paternity leave plays a significant role in supporting the mother's transition back to work, allowing for shared responsibilities and reducing stress.

FINAL THOUGHTS

CONCLUSION
ACKNOWLEDGMENTS
GLOSSARY
END NOTES

CONCLUSION

Right now, we are on the precipice of something great in tech sales. We are entering into a new era of technology and growth; with the rapid evolution of artificial intelligence and automation, quantum computing breakthroughs, expansion of 5G and increased connectivity, and sustainable and clean tech. With each advancement, tech becomes more and more desirable as an industry to work in.

We are seeing grass shoots of change, with women increasingly coming into sales roles and excelling. We are seeing them rise through the ranks, and becoming fantastic leaders who bring their teams to success.

At a societal level, too, we have seen advancements. Movements like #MeToo not only drew awareness towards issues of sexual harassment, but propelled discussions on workplace equity. This movement prompted many organizations to make efforts to address pay disparities, conducting pay equity assessments to ensure compliance and fairness. In the last decade in the UK, for example, the gender pay gap has fallen by approximately 25% for full-time employees. We also have seen improvements in DEI policies being brought to the table and driven forward, making necessary steps to improve diversity in organizations.

However, despite these advancements, there are signs of resistance to progress. In the US, for example, recent political actions have sparked concerns about the future of workplace equity. On January 20, 2025, President Donald Trump signed an executive order aimed at dismantling DEI programs within the federal government. This pushback serves as a reminder that the progress we've made is not guaranteed – ongoing commitment to change is essential.

Within the workplace, while more women are entering the pipeline, retaining them remains a challenge. Though entry level positions tend to be an equal split when it comes to gender, boardrooms and C-suites remain largely male (and white). A significant number of women who we spoke to at C-level were the only women in their organization at that level.

These shifts highlight the need for continued action. The momentum we've built over the past decade cannot be taken for granted – it is more important now than ever for us to support women at every level.

Through research and shared experiences in this book, we've highlighted not only why this is an industry worth joining and how women can progress, but also the significant impact that inclusive practices have on company culture and performance. When organizations support women effectively, the benefits extend far beyond individual careers, driving positive change across the entire business. Our goal is to showcase what works and inspire meaningful progress.

Women can be tremendous sellers and great sales leaders, who leave indelible marks on their organizations and propel them to new heights. If companies want to continue to succeed in the coming years, it is self-evident that they need to invest in women and in making their organization more diverse generally.

To enact real and meaningful change, attracting and retaining more women in sales needs to be a priority at both a board and

ELT (Executive Leadership Team) level. We have talked about how driving change from the top down is essential, but we cannot overemphasize it!

One way this happens is with policy changes. Individuals can advocate for changes to maternity policy, or better diversity company-wide, but if people at the upper echelon are not on board, it will not make the true impact that it needs to.

However, it isn't just about policy changes – it's about how the organization leads and hires, and how high DEI is on the agenda. Change does not happen organically, it has to be driven intentionally, with consistent work.

As we reach the end of *The Female Sales Leader*, we hope this book has not only highlighted the incredible opportunities in technology and software sales but also provided practical steps for women to thrive in these roles. Sales is a dynamic, financially rewarding, and flexible career that plays to many women's strengths. Yet, success requires more than just talent – it demands the right support, mentorship, and an environment that fosters inclusivity.

For women looking to advance, having allies, mentors, and the confidence to advocate for themselves is key. For organizations, the responsibility is clear: hiring practices must evolve, executive teams must champion diversity, and workplace cultures must actively support women's growth.

Change won't happen overnight, but together, we can shape a future where more women step into leadership, drive revenue, and redefine what success looks like in sales.

The path is there – now it's time to walk it.

ACKNOWLEDGMENTS

LUCY: Bringing this book to life has been an incredible journey, and I am deeply grateful to those who have made it possible. As an avid reader, writing a book has been on my bucket list since I was a young girl, where my love for reading and books was fueled by my Grandpa Ken.

I would like to say a massive thank you to the MEDDICC team, for not only believing in this work but for your unwavering support in bringing this to life. Robin, you have the patience of a saint, and all this would not have been possible without you. The weekend calls, the edits and the constantly changing our minds, as we wanted it to be perfect – you were key to this! Andy, Jess, what can I say, from that first meeting in our black roll necks to now, we have come such a long way and made something that hopefully will help many for years to come.

To my family and friends, whose encouragement has been my foundation – your love and belief in me has made all the difference. I know my dad would have been super proud of me, it was just before he passed away I told him of the project I was involved in and two years later we have done it.

My husband Aj, my partner in crime and biggest cheerleader, thank you for standing by me through every late night, every re-write and for being the sounding board I needed. And to my dog Beau, whose presence has been a constant source of comfort and joy, reminding me to take breaks and appreciate the simple things – playing ball.

Marina, Penny, we will be forever linked and I could not imagine doing this with anything else. Not only do we have a book, we have a friendship that will last for life.

But beyond gratitude, I want to leave a lasting message. Elevating women in the workplace, especially in the tech and tech sales – is not just a mission; it's a necessity. The future of innovation depends on diverse voices, bold leadership, and a commitment for breaking barriers. May we continue to push forward, lift each other up, and create a space where talent, ambition, and drive are respected , recognized and rewarded, no matter who you are.

This book is for every woman who has been told she couldn't and for every person committed to proving that she can.

MARINA: Had I told any of my school teachers that I would someday write a book, they wouldn't have believed me. This journey has been an incredible experience, fueled by the amazing people I've encountered and the time we've spent together. To everyone who has supported me along the way, thank you!

I owe a debt of gratitude to the MEDDICC team. Your patience and support have been invaluable, especially given our collective tendency towards strong opinions! The work you're doing at MEDDICC is truly inspiring, and I believe it offers an unparalleled foundation for anyone seeking a base in world-class sales training.

A special thank you to Penny and Lucy. I couldn't imagine having embarked on this journey with anyone else.

I am deeply grateful to the incredible women, family members, and male allies who have supported my career. You've believed in me when others may not have, challenged me to grow, and opened doors to opportunities I never imagined. I would especially like to thank Jason, Isi, Mark, Espen, and Josh, whose mentorship has been instrumental in my journey thus far.

And to my parents, whose unwavering support and sacrifices have paved the way for all my accomplishments. Thank you for instilling in me the values of hard work, resilience, and unwavering determination. You are my greatest role models, and I strive to embody the style, kindness, drive, and electric energy that you both exemplify in everything I do.

To everyone who has read this far, thank you! I hope these words have inspired you to pursue your own ambitions with passion and determination.

PENNY: Writing The Female Sales Leader has been a journey of reflection, growth, and purpose, and I am hugely grateful to those who have supported it. To the MEDDICC team – your dedication to this project and its broader mission has been incredible. A special thank you to Robin, our content writer, whose patience and commitment over the past two years have been incredible.

I also want to acknowledge my Mum, who instilled in me the values of hard work, resilience, and independence – qualities that have shaped my career. Though she is no longer with us, but her determination, zest for life, and unwavering love for her family continue to influence me every day, and this book is, in many ways, a testament to the lessons she taught me about perseverance and self-belief.

To my husband, Marcus – your unwavering support, encouragement, and belief in me have been invaluable. You push me to aim higher, challenge myself, and embrace every opportunity. From co-parenting to brainstorming ideas, you have been my greatest champion, and I continuously feel grateful to have you in my life.

To my children, Max and Amelie- you are my inspiration for the future. As you both grow and begin to shape your own careers, I hope this book serves as a reminder that anything is possible with determination and the right support system. I hope you always believe in your capabilities and never feel limited in your ambitions, and may you both contribute to a world that fosters inclusivity and success for everyone.

I also want to thank you to the mentors, managers, family, and friends who have played a role in my journey, as well as to my incredible co-authors, Marina and Lucy, and all the contributors – writing this book alongside such awesome people has been an amazing experience and I am honoured to have been able to collaborate with you on this.

Finally, to every woman aspiring to lead in sales, and every organization striving for inclusivity – this book is for you. May it serve as a guide and a source of encouragement, helping more women thrive in B2B software sales and beyond.

GLOSSARY

ACV – Average Contract Value

AE – Account Executive

ARR – Annual Recurring Revenue

BDR – Business Development Representative

CAC – Customer Acquisition Cost

Elevator Pitch – a brief, persuasive speech summarizing an idea, product, or service quickly.

ELT – Executive Leadership Team

ERG – Employee Resource Group

GTM – Go to Market; refers to the process of products being delivered to the customer

ICPs – Ideal Customer Profile; the perfect person or company to buy your product

LTV – Life-Time Value

MEDDIC/MEDDICC/MEDDPICC – a sales methodology. Stands for Metrics, Economic buyer, Decision criteria, Decision Process, Implication of pain, Champion and Competition

NPS – Net Promoter Score

NRR – Net Revenue Retention

OTE – On-Target Earnings

Playbook company – A company that provides structured strategies, best practices, and repeatable processes for business success.

Resume – a short description of your work experience and qualifications. Often referred to as a CV in the UK, but does not carry the same meaning as an academic CV in the US.

RSU – Restricted Stock Unit

RVP – Regional Vice President

SCIPAB – a communications framework that stands for Situation, Complication, Implication, Position, Action, Benefit

SDR – Sales Development Representative

SE – Sales Engineer

SVP – Senior Vice President

ENDNOTES

1   Krivkovich, A., Field, E., Yee, L., McConnell, M. & Smith, H. (2024) Women in the Workplace 2024: The 10th-anniversary report, LeanIn.Org and McKinsey & Company. https://www.mckinsey.com/featured-insights/diversity-and-inclusion/women-in-the-workplace p. 5

2   Software Sales Representative Demographics and Statistics in the US. Zippia. https://www.zippia.com/software-sales-representative-jobs/demographics/

3   Thomas, R., Fairchild, C., Cardazone, G., Cooper, M., Fielding-Singh, P., Noble-Tolla, M., Burton, A., Krivkovich, A., Yee, L., Field, E., Robinson, N., & Kuegele, S., (2023) Women in the Workplace 2023. LeanIn Org and McKinsey & Company. https://sgff-media.s3.amazonaws.com/sgff_r1eHetbDYb/Women+in+the+Workplace+2023_+Designed+Report.pdf p. 45

4   DiLorenzo Jr., L., Gill, J., Maguire, E., Smith, T., & Wilton, T. (2023, September 13). From tech investment to impact: Strategies for allocating capital and articulating value. Deloitte. https://www2.deloitte.com/uk/en/insights/topics/leadership/maximizing-value-of-tech-investments.html

5   Ibid.

6   Garibaldi, M., Husain, A., Madner, S. & Anil, N. (2023, July 10) Attracting and retaining tech talent to sustain mobility's growth. McKinsey & Company. https://www.mckinsey.com/industries/automotive-and-assembly/our-insights/attracting-and-retaining-tech-talent-to-sustain-mobilitys-growth#/

7   CompTIA. (2024). State of the Tech Workforce. CompTIA. https://comptiacdn.azureedge.net/webcontent/docs/default-source/research-reports/comptia-state-of-the-tech-workforce-2024.pdf?sfvrsn=a8aa5246_2

8   Scully, P. (2022, December 21). UK tech sector retains #1 spot in Europe and #3 in world as sector resilience brings continued growth. Gov.uk https://www.gov.uk/government/news/uk-tech-sector-retains-1-spot-in-europe-and-3-in-world-as-sector-resilience-brings-continued-growth

9   Ibid.

10   Yasukochi, C. (2023, March 10) Tech Sector Attracted Bulk of U.S. Venture Capital Funding Last Year. CBRE. https://www.cbre.com/insights/briefs/tech-sector-attracted-bulk-of-us-venture-capital-funding-last-year

11   Singla, A., Sukharevsky, A., Yee, L., Chui, M. & Hall, B. (2024, May 30). The state of AI in early 2024: Gen AI adoption spikes and starts to generate value. McKinsey. https://www.mckinsey.com/capabilities/quantumblack/our-insights/the-state-of-ai p. 1

12   Richter, F. (2022, May 11). Farewell iPod: The Rise and Fall of an Icon. Statista. https://www.statista.com/chart/10469/apple-ipod-sales/

13   LinkedIn Corporate Communications. (2019, March 5). LinkedIn releases new report showcasing how gender impacts the candidate journey. LinkedIn. https://news.linkedin.com/2019/January/linkedin-releases-2019-gender-insights-report

14   Baskin, K. (2024, February 13). Breaking Through the Self-Doubt That Keeps Talented Women from Leading. Harvard Business School. https://www.library.hbs.edu/working-knowledge/breaking-through-the-self-doubt-that-keeps-talented-women-from-leading

15   Orlob, C. (2017, March 29) Women in Sales Break the Rules of Selling, Yet Still Outperform Men. Gong. https://www.gong.io/resources/labs/women-in-sales/

16   Criado Perez, C. (2019). Invisible Women: Exposing Data Bias in a World Designed for Men. Vintage, p. 171

17   Thompson, A. E., & Voyer, D. (2014) Sex differences in the ability to recognise non-verbal displays of emotion: A meta-analysis. Cognition and Emotion, 28(7), 1164-95, p. 1184

18   Zenger, J., & Folkman, J. (2020, December 30) Research: Women Are Better Leaders During A Crisis. Harvard Business Review. https://hbr.org/2020/12/research-women-are-better-leaders-during-a-crisis

19   Adler, N. J. (1997) Global Leadership: Women Leaders. Management International Review, 37(1), 171-196, p. 184

20   Empathic leaders drive employee engagement and innovation.
(2021, September 14). Catalyst.
https://www.catalyst.org/about/newsroom/2021/empathic-leaders-
drive-employee-engagement
21   Xactly Corporation. (2019) 2019 State of Gender Equality in
Sales. Xactly. <https://www.xactlycorp.com/sites/default/files/file/2021-
12/gender-equality-sales-2019-xactly-min.pdf> p.3
22   Perez, p. 171.
23   Mumford, T. V., Campion M. A., & Morgeson, F. P. (2007).
The leadership skills strataplex: Leadership skill requirements across
organizational levels. The Leadership Quarterly, 18(2), 154–166, p. 158
24   Dawson, L. M. (1992) Will Feminization Change the Ethics
of the Sales Profession? Journal of Personal Selling & Sales Management, 12(1), 21-32, p. 21
25   Adler, p.178
26   Alliance for Board Diversity and Deloitte. (2023, June 15).
Missing Pieces Report: The 2018 Board Diversity Census of Women
and Minorities on Fortune 500 Boards. Deloitte, p. 9
27   Hunt, V., Layton, D. & Prince, S. (2015, January 1). Why
diversity matters. McKinsey & Company. https://www.mckinsey.com/
capabilities/people-and-organizational-performance/our-insights/why-
diversity-matters
28   Krivkovich, A., Field, E., Yee, L., McConnell, M. & Smith, H.
p. 5
29   Zippia.
30   Ibid.
31   Ibid.
32   Thomas, R., Fairchild, C., Cardazone, G., Cooper, M., Fielding-Singh, P., Noble-Tolla, M., Burton, A., Krivkovich, A., Yee, L.,
Field, E., Robinson, N., & Kuegele, S., (2023) p. 45
33   Krivkovich, A., Field, E., Yee, L., McConnell, M. & Smith, H.
p. 8
34   Thomas, R., Fairchild, C., Cardazone, G., Cooper, M., Fielding-Singh, P., Noble-Tolla, M., Burton, A., Krivkovich, A., Yee, L.,
Field, E., Robinson, N., & Kuegele, S. p. 10
35   Hunt, V., Layton, D. & Prince, S. (2015, February 2) Diversity
Matters. McKinsey & Company, https://www.mckinsey.com/insights/
organization/~/media/2497d4ae4b534ee89d929cc6e3aea485.ashx p. 7
36   Thomas, R., Fairchild, C., Cardazone, G., Cooper, M., Field-

ing-Singh, P., Noble-Tolla, M., Burton, A., Krivkovich, A., Yee, L., Field, E., Robinson, N., & Kuegele, S. p. 14

37   Ibid., p. 15

38   Ibid.

39   Deloitte's Center for Technology, Media & Telecommunications (TMT Center). (2023) 2023 technology industry outlook. Deloitte. https://www.deloitte.com/an/en/Industries/tmt/perspectives/technology-industry-outlook.html

40   The Language Women Use in the Workplace and What it Means. (2021, March 19). STEM Women. https://www.stemwomen.com/the-language-women-use-in-the-workplace-and-what-it-means

41   Wanted: More Women in Sales. (2020). Gartner. https://www.gartner.com/en/sales/trends/gender-diversity-in-sales

42   Narisetti, R. & Nordell, J. (2022) Author Talks: How to remove unconscious bias from the workplace, McKinsey & Company. https://www.mckinsey.com/featured-insights/mckinsey-on-books/author-talks-how-to-remove-unconscious-bias-from-the-workplace

43   Ibid.

44   Ibid., p. 17

45   Criado Perez, p. 98

46   Ibid., p. 93

47   Ibid.

48   Krivkovich, A., Field, E., Yee, L., McConnell, M. & Smith, H. (2024) Women in the Workplace 2024: The 10th-anniversary report, LeanIn.Org and McKinsey & Company. https://www.mckinsey.com/featured-insights/diversity-and-inclusion/women-in-the-workplace, p.37

49   Thomas, R., Fairchild, C., Cardazone, G., Cooper, M., Fielding-Singh, P., Noble-Tolla, M., Burton, A., Krivkovich, A., Yee, L., Field, E., Robinson, N., & Kuegele, S. p. 18

50   Ibid., p. 19

51   Krivkovich, A., Field, E., Yee, L., McConnell, M. & Smith, H. p. 42

52   TEDx Talks. (2016, February 1). Are you one of us? What behavioural science reveals on inclusion | Octavius Black | TEDxSquareMile. [Video] Youtube. https://www.youtube.com/watch?app=desktop&v=mOlynlKPR-8

53   Vial, A. C., Muradoglu, M., Newman, G. E, & Cimpian, A. (2022) An Emphasis on Brilliance Fosters Masculinity-Contest Cul-

tures. Psychological Science, 33(4), 595-612. https://journals.sagepub.com/doi/full/10.1177/09567976211044133

54   Sullivan-Hasson, E. (2021, March 8). TrustRadius 2021 Women in Tech Report. TrustRadius. https://solutions.trustradius.com/buyer-blog/women-in-tech-report/

55   Criado Perez, p. 277-8

56   Thomas, R., Cooper, M., McShane Urban, K., Cardazone, G., Noble-Tolla, M., Mahajan, S., Edwards, B., Yee, L., Krivkovich, A., Rambachan, I., Liu, W., Williams, M., Robinson, N., & Nguyen, H. p. 13

57   Ibid.

58   Criado Perez, p. 108

59   KPMG. (2020) Advancing the Future of Women in Business: A KPMG Women's Leadership Summit Report. KPMG, p.6

60   Ibid., p. 2

61   Ibid., p4

62   Ibid., p.2

63   Hardy, J., Roberts, R. & Hardy, L. (2009) Awareness and Motivation to Change Negative Self-Talk. Sport Psychologist, 23(4), 435-450, p. 436

64   Grenny, J., Patterson, K., McMillan, R., Switzler, A. & Gregory, E. (2023). Crucial Conversations (3rd ed.). McGraw Hill, p. 3

65   Rights during maternity leave and return to work. Maternity Action. https://maternityaction.org.uk/advice/discrimination-during-maternity-leave-and-on-return-to-work/

66   Rollins, M., Rutherford, B. & Nickell, D. (2014). The role of mentoring on outcome based sales performance: A qualitative study from the insurance industry. International Journal of Evidence Based Coaching and Mentoring, 12(2), 119-133, p. 119

67   Ibid., p. 125

68   Hunt, V., Dixon-Fyle, S., Huber, C., del Mar Martinez Marquez, M., Prince, S., & Thomas, A. (2023, December 5) Diversity matters even more: The case for holistic impact. McKinsey & Company. https://www.mckinsey.com/featured-insights/diversity-and-inclusion/diversity-matters-even-more-the-case-for-holistic-impact

69   Rock, D., Grant, H., & Grey, J. (2016, September 22). Diverse Teams Feel Less Comfortable – and That's Why They Perform Better.

Harvard Business Review. <https://hbr.org/2016/09/diverse-teams-feel-less-comfortable-and-thats-why-they-perform-better>

70   Hunt, V., Layton, D. & Prince, S. (2015) Why diversity matters. p.1

71   Ibid.

72   Wang J., Cheng, G. H. L, Chen T., & Leung, K. (2019). Team creativity/innovation in culturally diverse teams: A meta-analysis. Journal of Organizational Behavior. 40(6), 693-708, p. 701

73   Yang, Y., Tian, T. Y., Woodruff, T. K., Jones, B. F. & Uzzi, B. (2022) Gender-diverse teams produce more novel and higher-impact scientific ideas. PNAS, 119(36), p. 5

74   Hunt, V., Layton, D. & Prince, S. (2015) Diversity Matters. p. 9

75   Ibid.

76   Baker, M. (2020, August 10). 3 Actions to More Effectively Advance Underrepresented Talent. Gartner. https://www.gartner.com/smarterwithgartner/3-actions-to-more-effectively-advance-underrepresented-talent

77   What is psychological safety? (2023, July 17). McKinsey & Company. https://www.mckinsey.com/featured-insights/mckinsey-explainers/what-is-psychological-safety#/

78   Ibid.

79   Travis, D. J., Shaffer, E. & Thorpe-Moscon, J. (2019, November 21) Getting Real about Inclusive Leadership: Why Change Starts With You. Catalyst. https://www.catalyst.org/research/inclusive-leadership-report/

80   Thomas, R., Cooper, M., McShane Urban, K., Cardazone, G., Noble-Tolla, M., Mahajan, S., Edwards, B., Yee, L., Krivkovich, A., Rambachan, I., Liu, W., Williams, M., Robinson, N., & Nguyen, H. p. 37

81   Ibid., p. 14

82   Ibid., p.16

83   Devine, P. G., Forscher, P. S., Cox, W. T. L., Kaatz, A., Sheridan, J. & Carnes, M. (2017) A gender bias habit-breaking intervention led to increased hiring of female faculty in STEMM departments. Journal of Experimental Social Psychology, 73, 211–215, p. 213

84   Patel, S. (2023, February 24). Women in Sales: How Female Leaders Are Empowering the Sales Industry [2024 Data]. Mailshake. <https://mailshake.com/blog/women-in-sales/#:~:text=Female%20sales%20leaders%20only%20make,which%20have%20fewer%20

than%2030%25>

85   Kerr, G., & Pollack, A. (2022, January 19) Engaging Men: Barriers and Gender Norms. Catalyst. https://www.catalyst.org/research/engaging-men-barriers-norms/, p. 4

86   Thomas, R., Cooper, M., McShane Urban, K., Cardazone, G., Noble-Tolla, M., Mahajan, S., Edwards, B., Yee, L., Krivkovich, A., Rambachan, I., Liu, W., Williams, M., Robinson, N., & Nguyen, H. p. 27

87   Ibid.

88   Ibid.

89   Ibid.

90   Gaucher, Danielle and Friesen, Justin. "Evidence that Gendered Wording in Job Advertisements Exists and Sustains Gender Inequality." Journal of Personality and Social Psychology, vol. 101, no. 1, 2011, p. 109

91   Tockey, D., & Ignatova, M. (2019) Gender Insights Report: How women find jobs differently. LinkedIn Talent Solutions. <https://business.linkedin.com/content/dam/me/business/en-us/talent-solutions-lodestone/body/pdf/Gender-Insights-Report.pdf> p. 10

92   Criado Perez, p. 5

93   Ibid.

94   Gaucher and Friesen, p. 119

95   Ibid.

96   Criado Perez, p. 110

97   Gaucher & Friesen, p. 119

98   Tockey & Ignatova, p.7

99   Tockey & Ignatova, p. 9

100   Ibid.

101   Carlsson, M., & Eriksson, S. (2019). In-group gender bias in hiring: Real-world evidence. Economics Letters, 185, p. 2

102   Criado Perez, p. 111

103   Lucas, B. J., Giurge, L. M., Berry, Z. & Chugh, D. (2021, February 16) Research: To Reduce Gender Bias in Hiring, Make Your Shortlist Longer. Harvard Business Review. https://hbr.org/2021/02/research-to-reduce-gender-bias-in-hiring-make-your-shortlist-longer

104   Kerr & Pollack, p. 2

105   Ibid. p. 4

106   Gratwohl, N. (2023, June 1). «Attacked, outsmarted»: Why some men struggle with women on management boards, and why

female executives so frequently resign. NZZ. https://www.nzz.ch/english/why-do-male-executives-feel-threatened-by-women-colleagues-ld.1740281

107   Ibid.

108   Ibid.

109   Gartner (2020).

110   Criado Perez, p. 95

111   Gallo, A. (2023, February 15) What Is Psychological Safety? Harvard Business Review. https://hbr.org/2023/02/what-is-psychological-safety

112   Ibid.

113   Government Equalities Office. (2019, October 22) Employment Pathways and Occupational Change After Childbirth: Infographics. Workplace and Gender Equality Research Programme. https://www.gov.uk/government/publications/employment-pathways-and-occupational-change-after-childbirth

114   Criado Perez, p. 78

115   Ibid., p. 78-79

116   Gartner (2020)

117   Correll, S. J., Benard, S., & Paik, I. (2007). Getting a Job: Is There a Motherhood Penalty? American journal of sociology, 112(5), 1297-1339. https://gap.hks.harvard.edu/getting-job-there-motherhood-penalty

118   Ibid.

119   Deloitte. (2024) Women @ Work 2024: A Global Outlook." Deloitte Global. https://www.deloitte.com/global/en/issues/work/content/women-at-work-global-outlook.html p. 28

120   Ibid.

121   Criado Perez, p. 76

122   Criado Perez, p. 84Ibid., p.4

www.ingramcontent.com/pod-product-compliance
Lightning Source LLC
Chambersburg PA
CBHW040915210326
41597CB00030B/5088